The Other Side of Money

Living a More Balanced Life
Through 52 Weekly Inspirations

ISBN 978-0-9884316-0-7

52 Weekly Inspirations

It is a great honor to dedicate this book to my beloved husband.

Ric always loves and supports me as I grow and change in

the 35-plus years we have been sharing our lives.

Foreword

It was the first day of my sophomore year at college. I was sitting uncomfortably on the stage of Wilson Concert Hall. Sitting on my left was Mark Chamberlain, the president of Glassboro State College. On my right was Wayne Hoffner, the dean of students.

Seated in front of us, in the orchestra seats and up in the balcony, along the stairs and on the floor, was the entire freshman class.

It was Freshman Orientation, and it was 10 a.m. Time to officially welcome the frosh to their new lives as college undergrads.

As president of the sophomore class, I was required to join Mark and Wayne (I'll pretend we were buds) in speaking that morning. I was to greet the freshman class with a rousing speech. Be encouraging, I was told, assume the role of older brother. Be funny, be reassuring to these fresh new faces.

Dr. Chamberlain spoke, eloquently as I recall, as college presidents do. He then introduced me.

This is no way to start my sophomore year of college, I remember thinking. At least my jeans were torn — this was 1977, after all, and rebelliousness was still *de rigueur*, even if I was born a tad too late to join the '70s antiwar protests that my brothers got to enjoy.

It was legal for 18-year-olds to drink back then. Which means that nearly 2,000 kids were sitting in a hot auditorium hungover from their first night on campus, waiting for me to speak.

And they were thinking, this is no way to start my freshman year of college.

I started off with joking references to last night's drinking and idiot roommates, and then went into my sales pitch. The biggest event of the fall semester was a fundraiser called Project Santa. An 80-hour radiothon, it involved pretty much the entire campus, requiring 600 volunteers. Students would call the campus radio station to make a pledge. But it wasn't as simple as donating a dollar. No, students would pay a dollar *only if their roommates would go on stage at the Student Center and dance with a puppet in front of the entire student body.* Or something equally stupid. This pledge would require a volunteer to find and drag the roommate to the Student Center, force a performance, then go find the student who had made the pledge and get the dollar. In the days before cell phones and the Internet, this required hundreds of students to run all over campus looking for pledgers and pledgees. And all this went nonstop (it was easiest to find people at 2 a.m.) for nearly five days.

And as president of the sophomore class, I was in charge of the entire project.

So, I told of zany incidents the previous year: a student threw a pie in Dr. Chamberlain's willing face; the football team tossed a football nonstop for the entire 80 hours; a backpack worn by a student supposedly headed to the moon accidentally exploded on stage, to everyone's delight except for the Board of Trustees who were meeting downstairs, and so on. I urged all the freshmen to get involved. It's the best student activity on campus. Far more fun than any student club. You'll get to meet lots and lots and lots of people. And we collect money, food, clothes and toys for the needy. So come to a special meeting I'm hosting TODAY at the Student Government Association's office. I'll tell you about it and all the different ways you can get involved! See you there!

I stopped, they applauded, and I returned to my seat.

A couple of hours later, I stood in SGA's office, ready to greet the multitude. Would the room be big enough to hold everyone who would be coming?

Only one person showed up. Jean McMenamin.

And so began my love affair with her.

Jean became an essential part of what would be the most successful Project Santa ever. She went on to become president of her sophomore class, and she was reelected as president of her junior class. And then she did something no other woman had ever done: in her senior year, she was overwhelmingly elected president of the Student Government Association, the first woman ever to hold that position in the college's 58-year history.

And then, at the end of her senior year, Jean was bestowed with the college's highest honor: the Distinguished Senior Award, presented to only one graduating student each year. (No, I didn't receive it the prior year. Thanks for asking.)

Jean's popularity on campus was both obvious and unavoidable. It wasn't merely that she was likable, or devoted to student issues, or a hardworking, studious undergrad. There was more to it, and more to her, than that.

Jean exudes a special warmth that makes you glad she entered the room. You know immediately and instinctively that she is genuinely interested in you, that she cares who you are and what you want to say. She assumes responsibilities without being asked, removes burdens from others by taking them on herself, and she relishes in doing so.

And she's always smiling. Her empathic demeanor comes naturally to her, and when you meet her you're convinced that Jean truly believes that you are the only person in the world.

We've been together since her very first day at Glassboro in 1977. We've been a couple since 1978. She graduated in 1981, a year after me, and we got married in 1982.

We decided in 1986 to start a financial planning and investment management firm, after we sought advice from a financial advisor. That was a disastrous experience, so we decided to teach ourselves how to do it, so we could then share with others what we'd learned.

Our plan was simple: I'd focus on the education and advice, and Jean would do…everything else. So, she became our fledgling firm's first receptionist, bookkeeper, portfolio record-keeper, payroll and HR expert, IT technician, operations specialist and facilities manager.

In other words, with the exception of our financial planners, all 300 of our employees are doing jobs today that were initially (and solely) performed by Jean. These days, her role is Office Mom, and she continues to serve as the cultural foundation of the firm.

Jean's side of the business has always been a bit different. But not merely because our tasks were different. More fundamentally, it was this: while I focused on our clients' financial lives, Jean focused on their emotional lives. Clients would routinely arrive for appointments early so they could spend time with Jean before seeing me. They'd call just to chat with her, and more than one noted that our firm was named for her, not me.

The fascinating thing is that you'd never guess Jean's focus by reading her résumé. In addition to her natural leadership abilities, Jean's degree is in nutrition and consumer economics. She has always focused on the human side, the personal side. I can't remember the first time she said that our business is more *personal* than *finance*.

Indeed, as we know from our own experiences, there's more to life than money. And Jean has that unique talent of recognizing that money doesn't buy happiness, and that achieving peace and harmony within yourself and with others requires something more than merely maximizing investment returns.

So while most people engage in the rat race, ever striving to seek peace and balance by keeping up with the Joneses, Jean teaches us that it's not about things. It's about communication, laughter, walking dogs, reducing stress, taking time to listen, showing acceptance, and finding bliss.

So while I thought we were building an organization devoted to the accumulation and management of money, Jean has taught me that there is something much more important about money. It's easy to understand what that is. Jean shows us that we only have to look for it.

And the funny thing is, it's right in front of us. You'll find it right here — in *The Other Side of Money*.

~*Ric Edelman*

Introduction

When Ric and I started our business over 25 years ago, we made a promise to each other that we would make a difference. My degree from Glassboro State (now Rowan University) is in home economics, consumer economics, marketing and nutrition. For me, personal finance has always been more *personal* than *finance*. In all the jobs I'd had before we started Edelman Financial, I was always aware of how customers were treated, and it always bothered me when someone was not treated well.

So when we started our business, I was able to apply my college studies and create with Ric the principles upon which we built our business. We wanted our clients to feel at home, welcome and well cared for when they walked in our door. It all started with a smile and a dedication to do the right thing.

Ric and I are well matched. He is the visionary, and I'm the ground rod that keeps our lives in balance. For us, it's never been about the money. It's about doing the right thing. I guess our message and approach have resonated with people, because our little company is not so little anymore.

I remember the days when it was just Ric and me. He did all the financial planning and investing for each client, and I did...well, I did everything else. In the beginning I was the front office, the back office and everything between. I was the person who handled all the daily details to make sure each client was happy. Today, we have more than 300 employees in 31 offices who do what I used to do. It's fun to look back on it all.

Officially, my job was to make sure the office was running smooth-ly. But what I really did most of the time was get to know our clients and their families. Whenever they called, I was the one they talked to first. Whenever they visited, I was the one they saw first. And we'd spend a lot of time on the phone or in the lobby chatting before they'd meet with Ric. As I got to know them, I began to realize they were with us for more than just help with financial issues. We're supposedly a "money" firm, but I learned pretty quickly that money isn't always the real reason they come to us. I realized, like they did, that money is just a tool, a resource to help them achieve what really matters: the chance to spend time with their families, retire and fulfill their dreams. But I also began to realize that what many of our clients were really seeking was *balance* in their lives. Our business, I realized, is not simply about money. It's also about helping people be happy and enjoy their lives.

Realizing this made me want to help on a different level. Ric had already started writing a monthly newsletter for our clients, so in 2003 I started writing articles for it. My inspiration was usually something I observed or something going on in my world. I like to look for the bigger messages in daily life. There is usually a lesson to be learned. I have found joy and relief in talking about those lessons. When trying to decide what to call my column, we quickly realized we were talking about an aspect of personal finance that no one in the financial field ever discussed but was always obvious to me — that there is indeed a *personal* side to personal finance.

The Other Side of Money talks about finding balance, finding quiet, turning inward to be in the moment, looking at our lives and the lessons we need to learn to become better people who live in the light of love and gratitude.

So, this book is a compilation of the many columns I've written over the past decade. Join me on a journey through its pages as we ask ourselves questions: What are we doing to make our lives rich and fulfilling? Are we tuned in to the people in our lives? Do we treat each other with respect? Are we taking care of our local envi-ronment and resources?

Inside, you'll find 52 chapters, each offering insights into areas of your life you may not have considered, filled with possibilities you may not have recognized. Read just one chapter each week, and spend the next seven days with it. You'll find that time enlightening and uplifting.

Explore and enjoy all that is around you no matter what your age. Smile as often as you can. Share in the joy of the little things, for it is the little things that stay with us and make us smile in those quiet moments of our day. The quiet moments connect us to each other, to nature and to our animals.

My wish for you is for you to know you are loved. Life is a wonderful journey, and I'm honored to share the journey with you.

At the end of each chapter you'll find lots of helpful tips and ideas, such as these:

Points to Ponder
Important points you should give yourself time to consider.

Notes to Notice
Key bullet points for you to remember throughout your day.

Try It and See
Simple suggestions on how you can incorporate new concepts into your daily life.

Words of Wisdom
Inspirational and motivational quotes from people whose names you'll recognize (and others who may be new to you).

Go Online
Websites where you can find more information.

Patience

Life has become so fast.

Once it was the norm to need hours to complete a task — to cook dinner, for instance. Now seconds are too long to wait.

We live in an "instant" world. We are no longer interested in process; we care only about results. The pace has left behind something very important: *patience.*

Patience is the ability to tolerate delay. It implies self-control. Its cousin is *tolerance.* Tolerance is acceptance, while patience lets us go with the flow. Both words are now foreign to us. We seem so intolerant, so impatient these days.

When we are impatient, we act as though our moment is more important than another person's. When we are impatient, our tolerance slips away. Both reveal themselves when we are behind the wheel of a car, when we are in line, when we are not where we'd rather be.

How do we bring patience back into our day? We just need to take a breath and consider what we are doing. How important is it, really? Think as though we are each in a little bubble. We can move about each day inside a rigid bubble that pushes others out of our way — or we can be inside a soft bubble that ebbs and flows with and around other bubbles with ease.

Think about the times when we are rushing about in the grocery store. Our cart is the bubble. When we are in a hurry, we might crash into others and block aisles — almost like an arcade's bumper cars. But when we are not acting rushed, our cart moves easily through the aisles and we complete our shopping without stress.

When we feel impatient or intolerant, breathe deeply and look up at the sky. See that big universe out there? We are just a speck. Reminding ourselves of that can help us stop and look at the people we encounter, be more patient with them and have greater tolerance. Having a better perspective on the bigger picture of life will help us be more patient.

Patience is important for a happy existence. Patience equalizes. Let's slow down our bubbles so we can see each other and enjoy the world around us.

Try It and See

List 3 areas in your life where a little more patience will help the situation. Keep notes and observe after a few weeks how things have changed.

_____

_____

_____

Words of Wisdom

"Learn the art of patience. Apply discipline to your thoughts when they become anxious over the outcome of a goal. Impatience breeds anxiety, fear, discouragement and failure. Patience creates confidence, decisiveness and a rational outlook, which eventually leads to success."

~Brian Adams, author of *How to Succeed*

Clear Communication Improves Quality of Life

Picture a calm pond. Now imagine tossing in a stone and seeing the ripples. The ripples represent what we think and say, our actions and moods. These words and actions ripple from our lives into the lives of others. Will those ripples be positive or negative?

When we communicate with others (in word or action), *how* we communicate is as important as *what* we communicate. It's important that our conveyance is received in a manner that is (a) as we intended it, and (b) positive or favorable. Too often people talk without regard to the fact that someone is listening. So, when we communicate, remember that the receiver plays a key role. Will he or she understand what we're saying? Will he or she draw the conclusion we are trying to convey? Most important, will our relationship with that person be improved as a result of this interaction? Here are some ways we can help ensure that what we say and do is received positively by others:

1. Stop. Take a moment to think through your message. What exactly are you trying to communicate? Make sure the message is clearly what you intended.
2. Take a breath and smile. Even if we don't feel like smiling, doing so can alter both our frame of mind and the way the message is received.
3. Is it best to send our message in person or via text, email, telephone or voice mail? As Marshall McLuhan said, "The medium is the message."
4. Think about our words and how the person will hear our message.

5. Ask the receiver to tell us what they heard so we can confirm that our message has been accurately received. The feedback will facilitate effective communication and reduce everyone's stress levels.

As difficult as it can be to make sure our words and actions have a positive effect, it's even harder to be positive when we are the recipient of someone else's negative words and actions. We will need to find a way to turn their negative output into our positive input.

Here are some ways you can do this:

1. **Don't react.** Instead, listen to what they say. Rather than responding, simply excuse yourself. Time is often an effective defuser.
2. **Never fight fire with fire**; remember that firefighters use water to extinguish blazes. So don't turn someone else's crisis into your own. Instead, calmly and patiently explain that the manner in which they are communicating with you is not acceptable and request that it be tabled to another time.
3. **Before responding, stop and listen** to what is being communicated to us. Often, people in conversations alternate from talking to waiting to talk instead of talking and listening.
4. **Be tolerant.** Let upset, angry people talk. Often, people just need to vent, and until they have the opportunity to do so, they can't get past the immediate crisis. Let people talk themselves empty, and know that, often, they're not talking to us; they are just venting, and we happen to be in the room. Don't get caught up in their emotions.
5. **Ask questions and seek clarification.** By letting them elaborate, misunderstandings fade and relationships improve.
6. **If we become upset by a communication, take a time-out.** Listen to some favorite music, take a walk or focus on an unrelated but pleasant task to help us shake off any negatives feelings we may have picked up.

By minimizing the release of negative output and resisting the tendency to internalize negative input, we will discover that our life will become happier, more fun and less stressful. By staying focused on positives, we will see more solutions and experience fewer problems in our daily life.

Let's remember to picture our words and actions as pebbles so that all our ripples are positive and happy.

Words of Wisdom

"The real art of conversation is not only to say the right thing at the right place but to leave unsaid the wrong thing at the tempting moment."

~Dorothy Nevill (1826-1913), English writer

Points to Ponder

Is it just me, or have you also noticed that some people are leaving their manners at home?

Yes, we live in a fast-paced world. We have become a beautiful blend of many cultures and trends, so it's more important than ever that we display civility and daily manners.

Manners are the invisible rules of daily engagement. They consist of "please" and "thank you" and small gestures of respect and kindness. They are the invisible guides to our daily interactions.

Daily manners include greeting, introducing others and expressing thanks and gratitude. Daily manners are common courtesies. They include the small gestures we use to show others respect. We hold a door open or let someone go ahead of us in line. We respect others' personal property and their personal space.

By displaying our manners, we show that we are aware of our surroundings and conscious of how our behavior affects those around us.

Look up when we are walking. Say hi. Open a door for someone. Help with packages. In line — whether at the grocery store or on the highway — let someone in front of us.

We need to acknowledge each other. We need to connect with one another in some small way each day. We cannot let younger generations display poor manners. If we encounter someone who is displaying bad manners, it is proper manners to delicately and quietly bring it to his or her attention so that he or she may learn from the encounter.

After all, we are all in this world together. And manners are the language of a connected society.

Is Stress Reducing
Your Quality of Life?

Stress is a physiological response to psychological, emotional or physical pressure. When we are stressed, our bodies think we are under attack and our adrenaline increases, sending more blood to the brain. When the danger is over, our blood levels return to normal.

But if stress is constant, our blood level remains high. If left unchecked, this can cause serious long-term problems — high blood pressure and depression, problems in relationships and in our jobs. When we are under stress, even ordinary problems can seem insurmountable, and the smallest of tasks seems daunting.

Although this information is nothing new, we often fail to recognize that we are under stress. We are so focused on what we must accomplish today that we don't realize the effect that stress is having on us.

As we rush from one thing to the next, it would be helpful to know that our biological clock beats according to the pace we live. If we are always in a hurry, our biological clock speeds up. If we feel we don't need to rush, our biological clock slows down. Time is a subjective experience that translates into a biological response. So, let's look at some ways we can slow down our biological clock and help reduce some of our stress.

It starts with something as simple as *breathing.* Just breathing more slowly sends healthy, bright-red blood cells to our brains. This is the best method to create calm. A slow, long breath also helps us with methodical, considered thinking. Long, smooth exhalations can help ease minor physical aches and tensions. Simple, whole-some breathing techniques can help relieve anxieties.

Another way to help reduce stress is to *focus* on the moment. While talking with someone, are we also making a shopping list in our head or planning the quickest route home or fretting about some-thing we have to do later today? Take a breath — better yet, take two, and focus on the moment, on the project at hand, on the person we are talking to. Bringing focus to our actions and shutting out the rest of the world can reduce our stress level.

Practice breathing and focusing. It won't be easy at first, but if we can train ourselves when a stressful moment comes up to take a deep breath instead of reacting, that is a good first step.

Try It and See

Stress is a psychological response to pressure. A simple way to reduce stress is to breathe deeply. Stop, sit comfortably and inhale for four counts and exhale for four counts. Repeat for a minute. A slow, steady deep breath can get us through any situation. Anytime we feel a situation coming on, stop, count our inhalations and exha-lations until we have control of our emotions.

For more, you can also check out *The Art of Breathing — Six Simple Lessons to Improve Performance, Health and Well-Being* by Nancy Zi. www.theartofbreathing.com and www.meditationworkshop.org

Words of Wisdom

"If you ask what is the single most important key to longevity, I would have to say it is avoiding worry, stress and tension. And if you didn't ask me, I'd still have to say it."

~George Burns (1896-1996), comedian

Focus Your Energy on What You Can Control

There is so much going on today that we have no control over — terrorism and the economy, just to name two. I don't know about you, but I've been finding it hard to focus and function at normal levels. I'm also finding it very easy to be downright cranky, and small irritations can even upset me. I didn't think all the talk of war, terrorism, market declines, the weather and whatnot was bothering me, but it really was.

The first positive thing I did was to realize this. After all, we can't fix a problem until we know we have one. So, after asking myself why I felt jittery, I realized that the daily news was getting to me. But how to fix it?

The answer, I found, was remarkably simple. Instead of fretting over things I could not control, I focused on things I could control. I began to rechannel my energies in three areas. Perhaps this method can help you, too!

First, I discovered I had too many unfinished projects. They were constantly nagging at me. So, I decided it was time either to complete them or discard them. Here's the approach I took.

The first thing I did was turn off the TV and listen to music or find a funny movie. Then I began my attack on the unfinished list:

1. I created a list of all things that needed my attention. I sorted the list by House, Office and Family.
2. I broke each project into parts and pieces. Make phone calls or order items. By doing this, my excuses evaporated and I was ready to complete each item. In a few cases, I discarded the project because I decided it was no longer necessary or completion was beyond my control.
3. With the remaining to-do list in hand, I assigned a realistic completion time for each item and then penciled in that time on my calendar — just as I would a doctor's appointment. Some projects required 10 minutes while others needed hours of attention over many days, weeks or months. But as Ric reminded me, you eat an elephant one bite at a time, and I found that making regular progress was itself satisfying.

Wow! Did I feel better after putting together this little road map. I felt lighter, and my shoulders stopped hunching up around my ears. Even though I had not yet actually started to complete any of the items on my list, just having it all organized gave me a great sense of accomplishment. I also discovered that some items that were floating around in my head as "I have got to do this" did not even show up once I started my list. They must not have been that important!

The second step was to make sure I was getting scheduled quiet time each day. I chose to start with 30 minutes. Interestingly, when I first wrote down that number, 30 minutes seemed like a long time. But then I began to identify spots on my calendar where I could fit in a quiet minute here and there, and soon enough I realized this goal was quite achievable. In the beginning I wasn't sure I'd really want or need so much quiet time, but I soon discovered how valuable it is. After emerging from my self-initiated cocoon, I found I could deal much better with the world outside.

It's easy to find quiet time once we seek it:

1. Turn off the radio and MP3 player while in the car. Quiet drive time is wonderful. Try it. You will like it.
2. Create a period of time during the day when you don't answer the phone or respond to texts or e-mails. Once we are done with our quiet time we can reply to them all.
3. Turn off the TV!

My third and final step was to do something that most of us find difficult: just say no! Indeed, forcing myself to remove items from the list was difficult at first, but soon it became liberating.

By cutting back, I found myself with more time to enjoy family and friends. With fewer to-do items, my stress level went down, and I began to feel calmer. It's a wonderful feeling, and feeling wonderful in the midst of the world's craziness is truly a goal worth seeking.

Words of Wisdom

"Everything is determined...by forces over which we have no control. It is determined for the insect as well as for the star. Human beings, vegetables or cosmic dust—we all dance to a mysterious tune, intoned in the distance by an invisible piper."

~Albert Einstein (1879-1955), father of modern physics

Try It and See

A Sample Focus Method

SUNDAY	MONDAY	TUESDAY	WEDNESDAY	THURSDAY	FRIDAY	SATURDAY
1 **Plan for the Week** (2 hrs) Compile notes, phone call list, errands, etc.	**2** OFFICE **Projects** (2 hrs)	**3** FAMILY **Holiday Commitments** (2 hrs) HOUSE **Phone Calls** (2 hrs)	**4** HOUSE **Pay Bills** (30 min)	**5** FAMILY **Plan Vacation** (2 hrs) HOUSE **Errands** (2 hours)	**6** OFFICE **Phone Calls** (2 hrs)	**7** HOUSE **Shopping** (2 hrs) FAMILY **Birthday Party** (4 hrs)
8	**9** **Quiet Time** (30 min)	**10**	**11** **Quiet Time** (30 min)	**12**	**13** **Quiet Time** (30 min)	**14**

The Laughter Remedy

I went to the doctor recently, and he prescribed a dosage of 15 minutes of laughter to be administered once each day.

Such a serious prescription for medicine can be very funny indeed. The University of Maryland School of Medicine released studies validating just such a prescription. Researchers examined the expansion capability of blood vessels, known as vasodilation. Apparently, blood flow decreases 35% after experiencing stress but increases 22% after laughter — leading researchers to conclude that 15 minutes of laughing is equivalent to a 15-minute workout.

The reason for this? Stress hormones prepare the body for "fight or flight" by suppressing the immune system and increasing the number of blood platelets. That, in turn, can create obstructions in arteries and constrict blood vessels, which raise blood pressure. Laughter provides a safety valve by shutting off the flow of those stress hormones: when we laugh, our bodies increase the production of natural killer cells that destroy tumors and viruses.

Laughter, as we all know, is a physiological response to humor. Laughter consists of two parts: a set of gestures and the production of a sound. When we laugh, the brain pressures us to conduct both of these activities simultaneously. When we laugh, our bodies perform rhythmic, vocalized, expiratory and involuntary actions.

Philosopher John Morreall believes the first human laughter may have begun as a gesture of shared relief at the passing of danger. The relaxation that results from a bout of laughter inhibits the biological fight-or-flight response. Laughter also may indicate trust in one's companions. Many researchers believe that laughter is related to making and strengthening human connections. The more laughter, the more bonding.

What makes us laugh? The incongruity theory says we laugh at things that don't normally go together. (Think of George Carlin's famous line "Hand me that piano.") The superiority theory refers to our reaction when someone else incurs misfortune. (Think of the slapstick comedy of The Three Stooges.) And the relief theory says that, when injected at the right moment, humor can allow a person to relieve pent-up emotions. (It seems strange to think of laughing at a funeral, but we all know how common — and comforting — it is to tell funny stories about the deceased. The release is most welcome and very healthy.)

We don't all laugh at the same things or as often as we used to. Preschoolers laugh up to 400 times a day, while adults chuckle only a few times. And our cultures and our communities dramatically affect what we view as funny.

So how do we bring laughter into our daily lives? Create time to relax. Find time to play games with family and friends — not competitive board games but party-oriented games meant to induce laughter. Gather with others to watch comedies instead of horror flicks or tearjerkers. And go out of your way to laugh out loud at the slightest opportunity. Too often we hold back out of some misguided sense of propriety.

Words of Wisdom

"Laughter gives us distance. It allows us to step back from the event, deal with it and then move on."

~Bob Newhart, comedian

Notes to Notice

The world is in turmoil. It always is, it always was and it always will be in turmoil. Much of that is beyond our control.

But none of that matters.

What we need to remember is that today's turbulence is temporary. But that knowledge can be lost when we feel overwhelmed.

So let's focus on the everyday tasks, moments and people that make up our day. Even when the world feels out of control, we can always take small steps toward happiness.

Try It and See

1. Spend more time outdoors. The beauty of nature reminds us of the bigger picture, and fresh air and deep breathing can relax the mind and boost the immune system.
2. Focus on household and family tasks. Cleaning is a great stress reliever. We may not be able to fix the world, but we can organize the garage or tackle that overstuffed closet.
3. Put less into the day instead of more. We will find that when the day is packed with activities and the stress is piled high, things don't go well. We will be able to handle more if there is less on our plate.

Take in the day and enjoy!

Go Online

Madan Kataria, M.D., observed that his patients' immune systems improved after laughing. So he created yoga classes where participants laughed continuously for 15 minutes. It wasn't long before he ran out of jokes, so he decided that people could laugh without them. And because laughter is contagious in a group setting, unprovoked laughter made it easier for participants to join in. Thanks to Dr. Kataria's work, there are now more than 1,500 yoga laughter classes across India and more than 100 in the United States. Want to join a class? Go to:

www.worldlaughtertour.com/sections/clubs/northamerica.asp

So, our prescription: find out what makes you laugh and then do that often. Life is short! Don't waste it being stressed and angry.

Laugh! Doctor's orders.

Moodddeerrraaatttiiiiooon

There are pockets of time during the year that we overspend, over-indulge and think of everyone except ourselves. There are pockets of time during the year that we easily go off our routine. Are we constantly creating expectations that are unattainable? This only sets us up for disappointment and discouragement.

Well, let's find a cozy, quiet place in the house, turn on our favorite music, sip a cup of hot tea, and grab a pad and pen. We are going to write down what we want to accomplish this year concerning such topics as travel, exercise and eating habits. And as we write out our goals, we are going to introduce a new word into everything we do, one that may make success easier.

Moderation

Moderation means staying within reasonable limits, not excessive or extreme: mild or calm, composure, constraint, coolness, fairness, patience, poise, quiet, reasonableness, steadiness, toleration. The concept is *balance.*

This one word can give us so much because it gives us control. We really do have the power to set reasonable limits. So let's see how we can incorporate this new word into our everyday lives.

Work

Yes, we are busy. Yes, there are never-ending demands on us, but you know what? Work will be there tomorrow. So:

- **Focus on prioritizing the work** — Exceptions will come up, but having a general plan for the day helps.
- **Focus on the work** — We hate those big projects, we dread starting them, but once we start, we are done before we know it.
- **Move through the work** — Once we begin something, finish it without interruption. To avoid fatigue, schedule breaks; a break is not an interruption of work if it is scheduled. Rather, it is *part* of the work.
- **Feel the accomplishment** — Decide "I will finish X" and then go home for the day satisfied.
- **Leave the work behind** — It will be waiting for you tomorrow.

With moderation, we set reasonable limits. Don't let work control you. Instead, control it by maintaining composure and patience.

Family

- **Set reasonable limits** — Don't feel you need to volunteer for *everything,* or your fairness, tolerance and patience will be constantly tested. Take a breath and stop to think before you respond.
- **Eating habits and exercise** — It's all about planning ahead, and moderation can help. Here's how:
    <u>Exercise</u> — Start by scheduling small doses into your week. Try a daily 15-minute brisk walk. Maybe you can bring your sneakers to work and walk during your lunch hour. That way you are not fighting to fit it in with your morning or evening schedule. With moderation, we can set a reasonable goal that's attainable.
    <u>Eating habits</u> — We don't need to starve ourselves, and we don't need to declare abstinence from our favorite treats. All we need to do is avoid overindulging. Eat light during the day (instead of *nothing*) and allow ourselves the pleasure of the occasional treat of our favorite food.

Saving

Don't have $100,000 to invest? That doesn't mean you should save *nothing*. We need to remember that pennies, nickels and dimes add up. Saving regularly — even moderate amounts — can help us achieve our financial goals. Ric will be proud of us this year.

Moderation helps us do this. Let's set reasonable goals for ourselves. We will be successful if we work at them a little bit at a time. We will find a new pep to our step when we incorporate moderation into our day.

Words of Wisdom

"Never go to excess, but let moderation be your guide."

~Marcus Tullius Cicero (106-43 B.C.), philosopher

Try It and See

Set Some Moderate Goals

What area of your life seems most out of balance?

_____

_____

_____

Where do you want to spend more of your time?

_____

_____

_____

Look at your calendar and create a pocket of time to help you
accomplish your goal.

_____

_____

_____

Enrich Your Life — Vary Your Routine

We are such creatures of habit that most days we don't even realize it. The routine is comfortable, and we love the feelings of security and familiarity it gives us.

But routine can also shut us down as if we are sleepwalking through our day. Life is meant to be experienced, so let's liven things up a little. It can be very easy to vary our routine. Here are some ways we can do this. Give these a try, and see how they add variety and novelty to your day.

1. Change our morning routine a bit.
2. Don't follow the news.
3. Listen to different music or programming while traveling in the car.
4. Take a walk before starting your day.
5. Drink tea instead of coffee in the morning.
6. Take a different route to and from work.
7. Vary lunch in some way. Eat with different people, try a new restaurant.
8. Have someone read you a bedtime story.
9. Read a book on a subject you've never explored.
10. Try a different ethnic restaurant for dinner.
11. Play a children's game with adults.
12. Do what it takes to complete all your errands during the week so you can devote the entire weekend to yourself and to your family.

13. Write a letter or poem to someone you care about.
14. Do something nice for a person who can't possibly reciprocate (such as a stranger you'll never see again).
15. Take the family on a spontaneous day trip.

By moving out of our routine, we will rekindle the fun of discovery. It will improve our flexibility and make us open to change. By letting the day's circumstances flow over us, we will react with anticipation instead of anxiety, a smile instead of clenched teeth. Letting ourselves be open to new stimuli and experiences can be uplifting. Create a list of routine busters and discover how many smiles we find in our day.

Words of Wisdom

"The universe is change; our life is what our thoughts make it."

~Marcus Aurelius Antoninus (121-180 A.D.), Roman emperor

"The only sense that is common in the long run is the sense of change — and we all instinctively avoid it."

~E.B. White (1899-1985), writer

"Nothing endures but change."

~Heraclitus (540-480 B.C.), Greek philosopher

Why Can't Every Day Be a Holiday?

If a magic genie appeared and gave me three wishes, my first wish would be for everyone to slow down enough to enjoy the moment. My second wish would be for everyone to see the gifts in their everyday lives. The third wish would be for everyone to appreciate their gifts, no matter how small they may appear to be.

The notion of these wishes occurred to me as I've thought (and continue to think) about the season I'm calling "The End of the Year." I was hyperobservant during the last two months of the year — watching family and friends whirling about in a frenzy to get things done. It became apparent to me that the commercialism of The End of the Year whips us up, turning us into cranky, exhausted individuals. When did we let the importance of the "thing" out-weigh the importance of the "person"? And why did we let that happen?

It isn't just about The End of the Year. It's also about Valentine's Day and all the other "holidays" that are exploited — if not downright created — by some marketing department. I'm supposed to show my husband on Valentine's Day that I love him? Really? I love my husband every day! Why do I have to do something special on that day? Why is there an assumption that I don't do this every day? And why must he believe there's a hurdle to overcome or a standard to meet or exceed for me? I refuse to buy into the flowers and choc-olate routine that is pushed on us every February 14th. If my husband doesn't spend money on flowers or chocolate, he doesn't love me? Really?

We are good to our family and friends every day of the year. We spend time with our family and friends throughout the year, creating fun memories. The End of the Year is not a hall pass allowing us to ignore our family and friends for 360 days, making up for it with a store-bought gift once a year. My gift-giving list consists of an entire year of talking and dinners and vacations and game nights and movie nights and phone calls and emails and texts and whatever else we can think of — each message, event and day is an expression of my simple message: I love you.

Do we really have to prove how we feel by buying something others can easily obtain for themselves? Do we really have to do that? And do we really have to do it on one specific day of the year?

Sure, there are traditions to maintain and etiquette that society wants us to follow. Giving gifts is fine, and setting aside a time for us all to take a moment to share these gifts can be wonderful. But when the effort to re-create life as it was in Bedford Falls does little more than add stress to our already-crazed lives, then we haven't gained anything; we've lost something.

Can we turn it all down a few notches? Can we find a way to reach The End of the Year with joy and calm instead of exhaustion and stress?

Let's start now with a new plan. Let's make every day a holiday. Let's share our love on all 365 days instead of just mentioning it on a couple of holidays each year.

Ask the genie within you to grant these three wishes.

Try It and See

List 3 things you can do to simplify year end.

_____

_____

_____

Do You Know
Why You Smile?

Smiling makes us happy, and when we're happy we smile. Smiling is contagious — see what happens when you approach someone with a smile on your face. Smiles can be heard on the phone — the person on the other end knows if we're smiling.

Smiling not only makes us feel good, it's good for us. People who smile are thinking positive, happy thoughts. Research by the Mayo Clinic found that "positive attitude yields positive, healthy results." A study by Yale University found that positive thinking even helps people live longer, happier lives. Smiling makes us happy, and being happy makes us healthier.

So let's do a happy health check! Be happy because of:

✔ **Everything we have.** Each morning, we awake to fresh air, with a roof over our head, with food to eat, clothes on our back, and family and friends. Want more? Great! Go after more! As you strive to do so, you'll find yourself smiling!

✔ **All our accomplishments.** Life is a wonderful, happy journey, and we've been through a lot in our lives. Think about all you've done and all you have yet to do! Consider the challenges you've faced and the road that lies ahead. Dissatisfied with your accomplishments to date? Great! Go achieve more! As you strive to do so, you'll find yourself smiling!

✔ **Our ability to laugh at ourselves.** We do funny, silly, stupid things all the time. We all do! It's what makes us human, so go ahead and laugh about them! If we take ourselves a bit too seriously, look in the mirror and smile at our reflection. It's fun!

Does all this sound silly? It's not. In fact, it's the happy truth, and we can happily prove it to ourselves. Just start smiling, and wonderful things will start to happen.

Notes to Notice

Before you go to sleep each night, take a moment to find a few highlights in your day. Smile, say thank you and enjoy a peaceful night's sleep.

Words of Wisdom

"Let us always meet each other with a smile, for the smile is the beginning of love."

~Mother Teresa (1910-1997),
nun, Missionaries of Charity, Nobel Peace Prize winner

What I Have Learned During 30 Years of Marriage

Ric and I have been blessed with 30 amazing years of marriage — and counting. So I thought it might be fun to impart some of the things we have learned.

1. Laugh, laugh, laugh!
2. Remember that it takes *work*. We both must bring 100% to the relationship.
3. Never stop dating each other.
4. Remember that the little things do count.

Communicate, communicate, communicate! Talk openly to each other. As the years go on, we continue to change. It is important to change together.

1. Never go to bed angry.
2. Have patience.
3. Never let the extended family interfere with the decisions we make as a couple.
4. Start each year by writing down goals — first as individuals, then joint goals we'll accomplish together.
5. Stay active together — play sports, exercise, bike, hike, swim, walk together.
6. Never lose our individuality. Continue to explore and develop our own hobbies and interests.
7. Be a good listener. Don't assume that we know what our spouse is going to say. Instead, *actively* listen.

8. Set aside times for ourselves. If we overextend ourselves by focusing on others' needs first, we can burn ourselves out pretty quickly.
9. Never stop learning about each other. As we grow older, we'll change — our habits, our preferences, our opinions. Our spouse is changing, too. Do we know who our spouse has become? Rediscover our spouse on a daily basis.
10. Learn to relax and do nothing together.

It takes a lot of work to have a happy marriage — and it's the most rewarding job to have.

Try It and See

Using the above list as a reference, what are 3 simple things that you could do (or stop doing) that would help you enjoy each other more? Write them down and share them with your partner.

_____

_____

_____

Create a list of 3 ways to find time in your day/week/month to have quiet time for just the two of you.

_____

_____

_____

The Four Legs to the Balanced Chair of Life

As the years keep clicking away I often ponder the mysteries of life. I wish to answer one question: How to create balance in life?

The search has led me to many books, trying to find the answer. Well, I'm happy to report that I have finally found the person and the book. Don't laugh, because it's a book about dogs, by Cesar Millan, called *Be the Pack Leader.*

The book begins with a reference to the film *Koyaanisqatsi,* which Ric and I first saw in the early 1980s and which we still talk about (and occasionally watch) some 25 years later. Based on the Hopi Indian word meaning "life out of balance," the film offers beautiful sequences and relaxing music while showing images of industry and technology to demonstrate that we have gotten out of balance with nature. Although the film is a bit dated today, its message is still powerful.

The film is an appropriate introduction to Mr. Millan's book. It gave me, to use a metaphor, the four legs of a chair. In order to have balance in life, we must focus on four areas: intellect, emotion, spirit and instinct. If just one of these is off kilter, the chair will fall over.

Intellect: Most of us tend to "live in our heads" — constantly thinking, living in a world of logic and reasoning. Being tethered to our electronics may seem natural, but it is not. We need to take a vacation from our heads and find a creative outlet.

Emotion: For a variety of reasons that we all know, we often hold back, refusing to express our emotions. But holding back can cause us to subconsciously develop extreme behaviors and even disease. Our bodies and minds will reach a point where they cannot hold it in anymore. The solution is to find outlets for our emotions so we can express them in a consistently healthy manner. Art and music are wonderful outlets.

Spirit: Being in touch with the deeper part of our being is essential, giving us a sense that we belong to something bigger than ourselves. It gives us a greater sense of the world and helps us see how we all fit in it together. Philanthropy, community and church help us connect with ourselves.

Instinct: We must be attuned to the signals we get from the world around us — our environment, people and animals. For most of us, this is the most dormant leg of our chair, and it is just waiting to be awakened. Most days, the intellectual mind keeps us from the instinctual self. So put away the electronics and get outdoors. Give our brain a rest in order for us to truly tune in to what is happening around us and really hear what people are saying to us.

I'm thankful to Mr. Millan for finally giving me a base on which to build my chair. Let's start by giving each leg 25%. Over time, we will get stronger in each area. Just having the awareness can help rebalance our chair and make sitting at the table of life much more enjoyable.

Words of Wisdom

"Allow yourself to yield, and you can stay centered.
Allow yourself to bend, and you will stay straight.
Allow yourself to empty, and you'll get filled up.
Allow yourself to be exhausted, and you'll be renewed."

~*The Tao Te Ching of Lao Tzu*, sage of the 6th century B.C.

The Zen of Laundry and Other Daily Chores

They are there every day — chores that nag at us, chores we know need to get done, constant clutter and dust. They never go away.

Rather than wearing us out, these daily tasks can rejuvenate us!

I'm not saying we should become a house-cleaning freak, but with the proper attitude, house cleaning can be very therapeutic. Just take on a task and see it through to the end.

For example, for me there is a great sense of accomplishment to get the laundry washed, dried, folded, ironed and put away in the same 24 hours. (Okay, so it really doesn't happen often, but I can dream, can't I?)

Just push away the external happenings of the day and focus on this one task, the sound of the washer, the smell of clean clothes as they emerge from the dryer, the quiet while folding clothes before putting them away. I love to use laundry time as my quiet time.

Grocery shopping is a big time killer. Too often it's last minute, often while we and others are hungry. So use some of your quiet time to take stock of what you have in the house. Then peruse a cookbook for new menu ideas. With your list in hand, head to the market — ideally, by yourself. Take a relaxing walk through the grocery aisles, even those you don't need to visit. Treat the time as yours. Being relaxed, we can use our cooking time as creative time and enjoy preparing a wonderful meal for those we love.

Another good way to be with our own thoughts is to engage in that greatest of mindless chores: vacuuming. Because it's a physical activity with a rhythm and pace, it's a wonderful time to practice our breathing. Use this time to mentally organize yourself, and when done, look at your accomplishment. There's nothing like looking at a newly vacuumed room. It just brings a smile. (At least until the kids and pets trample through!)

Dusting, cleaning windows, emptying the dishwasher...the list of chores goes on and on. My point is that we should look at them in a different way, use them to help us find a quiet moment — to think, be creative, feel good about a job well done.

And soon, we get to do it all over again!

Words of Wisdom

"It is not how much we have, but how much we enjoy what we have, that makes us happy."

~Charles Spurgeon (1834-1892), British preacher

"When we pay attention, whatever we are doing — whether it be cooking, cleaning — is transformed… We begin to notice details and textures that were never noticed before; everyday life becomes clearer, sharper and at the same time more spacious."

~Rick Fields (1942-1999), author of *Chop Wood, Carry Water*

Turn Those Catalogs Into a Collage of YOU

I've recently signed on as the pen pal for a child being served by an inner-city charity. As part of the process, I was asked to create a collage of myself to give the child a visual picture of who I am.

A picture of who I am. That sounded simple enough until I really thought about that question.

Who am I?

When's the last time you asked yourself that question? I have to admit, I got a little nervous, because it is a big question. After all, who am I? We all tend to throw ourselves into work and family, so we often forget about ourselves. It took some time for me to remember all those things that I enjoy being and doing.

Soon I was ready to create my collage.

I flipped through mail-order catalogs, and I asked myself:

- When I was a kid, what was fun for me?
- What do I like to do now?
- What is it I never have time for but would like to do?
- What are the new interests I am developing?

Then with these thoughts in mind, I looked for pictures to illustrate them.

Life is all about continually discovering and rediscovering who we are — reminding ourselves about what makes us happy.

What motivates us? What keeps us focused? What makes us tick?

The beauty is that our answers can change yearly, monthly, even daily. By giving ourselves a series of pictures of who we are, our goal of achieving happiness can come into focus.

There is nothing more grounding and satisfying than having a great sense of self. Have fun defining "us" and what makes us happy. We'll find ourselves more sociable, flexible and forgiving — and able to tolerate life's daily frustrations more easily.

Try It and See

Start a collage and make it a work in progress. All you need is:

- The catalogs that arrive in the mail every day
- Scissors
- A glue stick
- A large piece of construction paper or art board

Think about your collage. List 3 things you no longer do but you would like to find the time for again. Now look at your calendar and see if you can block time for your activities.

_____

_____

_____

Words of Wisdom

"I admit that thoughts influence the body."

~Albert Einstein (1879-1955), father of modern physics

Pondering the Puzzle of Life

When Ric travels, one of my favorite activities, after I tuck in our dogs for the night, is to grab a cup of tea and sit down with a beautiful puzzle. Now, this might sound like an extremely boring venture, but I enjoy the quiet. I like to take in the colors and shapes of the puzzle pieces. And as I worked on a puzzle recently, some life lessons popped into my mind:

Life is one big puzzle. At times it is hard to have the patience to let the pieces fall into place. But keep at it and be patient. Everything comes together in its own time.

Organizing all the pieces. We like life to be neat and organized. But scattering the pieces haphazardly across the table is fun. Being disheveled is really okay — let go once in a while and see how great it feels.

One piece at a time. While seeking a certain piece, it's easy for our eye to catch another, which can be tempting to try to place. Before I knew it, I had half a dozen pieces in my hands and wasn't getting anything done. Resist the temptation to take on too much at one time. Block out the desire to multitask. Instead, focus and finish one piece at a time. See how free it makes us feel.

Quiet. A warm cup of tea, relaxing music and a quiet puzzle: it's really all we need, and we all need it. Schedule time for ourselves to sit and sort through the puzzles of our life and prioritize our thoughts.

The simple pleasure of connecting the pieces. By slowing down, even the smallest accomplishment can feel monumental.

Change the view. When stuck or in a dilemma, look at the situation from a different perspective. Simply turning the pieces upside-down provided a completely new view and solutions suddenly revealed themselves. Turn things around and even upside down. You'll be amazed at how the new view helps us bring things together.

Life is a puzzle. Have fun with it!

Words of Wisdom

"I believe that we are solely responsible for our choices, and we have to accept the consequences of every deed, word and thought throughout our lifetime."

~Elisabeth Kubler-Ross (1926-2004), Swiss-American psychiatrist

Step Away From the Computer and No One Gets Hurt

As I was on my way home from work one night, I wondered, how many people did I interact with that day? It was a time of year with a deadline, and I had spent most of the day in front of the computer.

I looked back on my day and realized that I gave all my good energy to the computer. Wow, I don't think the computer appreciates the sacrifice I just made. Yes, I know computers are good and helpful and necessary to make our lives easier, but are they taking away human contact? Yes, I spoke to lots of people via e-mail. But with how many did I actually have a verbal exchange or even eye contact? Sadly, for this particular day, the answer was only two.

The machines reduce our ability to convey and receive emotion. We need to connect with each other. We are blessed with our human element, and we need to balance that against the electronics. Connecting with the Internet is fine, provided we also stay connected with people, the Earth and animals.

Here are some easy ways we can put the human element back into our daily lives:

- When the weather is nice, how about for every hour we sit in front of the computer, we give ourselves a five-minute walk. So if you work (or play) at the computer for eight hours, take a 40-minute walk.

- Join a friend or coworker for lunch. Lots of interesting interaction there.
- Have the kids set aside the electronic games. Play real, not virtual, games with them.
- Engage in some type of volunteer work that involves people. Visit a nursing home or hospital, spend time at a shelter, or read to kids at the library.
- Create or join a book club and meet with friends — new and old — once a month to talk and share (and maybe even discuss the book!).
- Get the kids outside. Create a garden together. Fly some kites. Hike in a park. Let the fresh air fill your lungs.

To sustain happy, healthy lives, we need lots of human interaction every day. The electronics are not the answer. Nothing can replace eye contact and verbal repartee. It is very important that we share this gift with younger folks who are growing up attached to electronics. We don't want them to grow up more comfortable with a computer than with people.

Let's find the balance and we'll find each other.

Try It and See

Find 3 pockets of time during the day that you can step away from your electronics. Take a walk, find something quiet to do.

Words of Wisdom

"It's all about quality of life and finding a happy balance between work and friends and family."

~Philip Green, British businessman

Have You Exercised Your Brain Today?

We all know that exercise is important to keep our muscles and bones strong. But did you know that your brain needs exercise, too?

If we plan on keeping our minds sharp as we age, we need to take care of our brains now. Proper maintenance can keep our memory sharp and our motor skills in good working order. Proper diet has a role, as do a healthy lifestyle and stress control.

The human brain has two sides. The left side controls our logical thinking, math, science and language skills. The right side is our creative side, allowing abstract thought, emotions and risk. Together, the two create our distinct personalities. We must exercise and develop both sides to keep our mind as sharp as possible.

Here are some daily steps to help keep our brains in tip-top condition:

Healthy diet: Every day, eat fresh fruits and vegetables that are rich in antioxidants. Tip: Focus on fruits and vegetables that are dark in color.

Lifestyle and less stress: Find time for ourselves. Plan and prioritize our day, and avoid over-scheduling. Try a yoga class!

Healthy brain activities:

1. Learn something new. Our brains crave knowledge. Every time we learn, we retain information, which helps us form neurons.

2. Keep our brain active. Turn the TV off, pick up a book or engage in stimulating conversation. Engage in more than one activity at a time. Multitasking has become common for most of us, but that's usually by accident or at the insistence of others. Take control of this exercise by selecting our own multiple activities, such as singing along with our favorite music while doing chores.
3. Play games. Word games, puzzles, board games, card games and many others are terrific at exercising our brain. Chess, of course, is the ultimate brain game.
4. Start a journal. Free-form writing encourages creativity, which is a great brain stimulator.
5. Take a walk. Physical activity is very important, for it boosts the brain's ability to process and retain information, thanks to increased circulation and blood flow to the brain. Go bird -watching or hunt for specific plants and learn a little something along the way.

We can all do this. We need to do this. Let's jump-start our brains today!

Try It and See

Pick 3 activities to add to your daily/weekly/monthly routine. Make note of how you feel after each activity — keep it up for 30 days and log your progress. Reevaluate your activity after the 30 days to see if you want to change, add or delete anything.

_____

_____

_____

Always Do the Right Thing

I was meeting Ric for dinner one evening and driving his sedan. I have driven it before, so it was not like I was unfamiliar with it. As I pulled into the parking spot I heard a noise. No — it could not be — did I touch the car next to me? I quickly got out, and yes indeed, I had scraped the car next to me.

Okay, now what? I did not have a pen or paper, so I ran into a nearby store to get paper, wrote a note explaining how sorry I was, added my name and telephone number, and placed it on the other car's windshield.

Then I waited to hear from the car's owner.

I was not sure what to expect, becuase nothing like this has ever happened to me. After three days, I received a phone call from a very appreciative, soft-spoken gentleman. He was gracious and complimented me for leaving the note. When I again apologized, he said, "Not to worry, there are bigger things in life to worry about." He had polished the scrape and merely asked me to reimburse him $17.85, the cost of touch-up paint.

I was shocked by his reaction and naturally very happy and relieved. He was equally happy, because he initially assumed that no one was going to take responsibility for the damage.

Footnote: After we exchanged e-mails, he realized who I was. It turned out that he is a client of our firm, and he and I live in the same community. It makes me even gladder that I did the right thing.

We all know that we should always do the right thing. And I certainly felt better for doing so. Now scientific evidence explains why!

The breakthrough was reported recently by neuroscientists at the National Institutes of Health. Volunteers were asked about a scenario involving either donating a sum of money to charity or keeping it. While they pondered the question, their brains were scanned. Researchers found that a primitive part of the brain that usually lights up the monitors when subjects are offered food — a part of the brain scientists call the "reward center" — was activated when subjects were being charitable. This demonstrates that people feel rewarded when being kind to others.

If we keep this in mind the next time we are confronted with a situation — such as my little incident with the parked car — the correct path will become very clear.

Words of Wisdom

"A life directed chiefly toward the fulfillment of personal desires will sooner or later always lead to bitter disappointment."

~Albert Einstein (1879-1955), father of modern physics

Notes to Notice

First, we need to remember the impact of our decisions. They affect every aspect of our lives. No action goes unnoticed. We may try to trick ourselves by thinking that our actions do not matter, especially if no one is watching. But these are the moments that count the most.

The moment we are faced with a choice we can ask ourselves the following:

1. Will this decision move me forward or keep me stuck in the past?
2. Will this action/decision bring long-term fulfillment or merely short-term gratification?
3. Am I being true to myself or am I just trying to please someone else?
4. Am I looking for what is right or am I looking for what is wrong?
5. Will this situation help me find personal growth or will I regret it?
6. Is this action/decision coming from a place of love or fear?

Ask the questions, listen to the small voice inside and we will find the right path. It is a small world, and we are all connected to each other.

Points to Ponder

I have been fighting with my hair all of my life. Well, actually, my mom fought with it in my early years, but then I took over. So, I recently went to yet another new hairdresser.

She said, "You have naturally wavy hair."

"Yes," I replied with a sigh, "but I can never get it to look smooth and straight."

She looked at me quizzically. "Why not go with your natural curl?"

I was stunned. How come I never thought of that!??!?!?

For years — decades! — I've been fighting with my hair to get it to do something it simply didn't want to do. Now in one easy salon visit, my hair has become sassy, empowering and fun. But if I had not been open to new ideas, I would not be enjoying the new me.

We need to be open to change. Opportunities that could change our life are right in front of us — if only we open our eyes to them.

It is healthier to not get stuck and rigid in our thinking. Life is constant change. Without change, we do not learn. We become bored, complacent, lazy and close minded. The test is how easily we can adapt to change.

Checking in daily on how we conduct our daily lives is an easy start. Can we do things better, faster, easier and cheaper and maybe add in some fun? What resources can help us?

Let's look at our daily routine. What changes can we make?

Go Online

To learn more, visit:
www.thelifechangenetwork.com
www.positive-changes-coach.com

The Power of Our Pets and What We Can Learn From Them

It is often after someone leaves us that we realize how they touched our lives. It is often when they are gone that we miss their strengths and reflect upon the lessons they taught us. It is in this light that I share some lessons our Liza brought to us. Yes, she was a dog, but she was very special to us.

Patience

Our pets are the epitome of patience. They wait for us all the time. To be fed, walked, played with. That is all they do — wait. Wait for us to make the time for them. They never get mad when we are late, busy or forgetful. They always understand. We need never ask them to forgive, because as far as they are concerned, there is never anything that needs forgiving.

We need to put this wonderful trait into our daily lives. We are in too much of a hurry, and too often we think our time is more important than someone else's. We can learn a lot from our pets about patience.

Communication

Even though they can't talk, it's easy to know what our pets are feeling — happy, sick, hungry, sorry (for whatever it was they did while we were away). It takes just a moment for our pet to immediately communicate their feelings. Pets are always anxious to let us know what is going on with them, and that's another lesson for us to take to heart. I'm not sure why, but many of us have stopped talking to each other. Living with animals has shown us the importance of communication. Learning how to formulate our thoughts and opinions, and how to share them effectively, is so very important. Our kids, spouse and coworkers need to know and understand us — not just what we have to say, but why we need to say it. We can each communicate more effectively.

Taking in the moment

Most days we have more than enough to do. We can't wait to finish whatever it is we're doing right now because we're already thinking about moving on to the *next* project. Not our pets. Our pets live in the moment; whatever they are doing is all there is. While taking a walk, they stop to notice the smallest bug, listen to the newest sound or absorb a scent from blades of grass. Instead of letting me push her forward, Liza taught me to linger, take a deep breath and slow down. Soon, I too learned to hear the birds and notice the clouds. These wise animals can help us learn to enjoy where we are and what we're doing — whatever and wherever that is. As a result, contentment emanates from everything they do. We should do likewise.

The "pack" is the most important thing

Dogs give great greetings, whether you've been gone five days or just five minutes. And as much as they express interest in whoever arrives at the door, they save their warmest greetings for their family. The ultimate pet lesson is the importance of family and celebrating being together. There is nothing better than spending time with those who are important to us, and our pets reinforce that notion every day.

You can never give or get enough kisses and hugs in a day

Animals are endless sources of love and kindness. The lesson: we must not take for granted those close to us. We tend to push ourselves to the limit most days, and we sometimes ignore those closest to us. But our pets would tell us the importance of demonstrating our love not just daily, but constantly.

Take time to learn from our pets. They have a lot to teach us.

Words of Wisdom

"Maybe journey is not so much a journey ahead, or a journey into space, but a journey into presence. The farthest place on earth to journey is into the presence of the person nearest you."

~Nelle Morton (1905-1987), activist for racial justice

"Do not dwell in the past, do not dream of the future, concentrate the mind on the present moment."

~Buddha (536-483 B.C.), spiritual teacher

Points to Ponder

Life is a gift — as we at Edelman Financial were reminded when a staff member was abruptly taken from us by a hit-and-run driver.

But is such a tragedy necessary to help us make the changes of slowing down and finding balance with ourselves, family and friends?

Every day, each breath, is a gift. Nothing is guaranteed. How differently would we conduct our day if we truly understood this gift of life? We certainly would not waste the day in a job we do not like or hang around people who get under our skin.

So maybe we can start the day by making time just for ourselves and committing to spend quality time with family or friends.

If we truly understood the gift of life, we would be happy to see everyone in our day. We would not waste time gossiping or being rude and self-centered. (We might even let someone in front of us while driving in heavy traffic.)

If we truly understood the gift of life, we'd see challenges and problems as opportunities for growth and movement forward.

If we truly understood this gift of life, no day would be without an "I love you" and lots of hugs and kisses.

Can we start today? Can today be the day it sinks in? Can today be the day we incorporate the balance? Can today be the day we begin to appreciate the small things in life? Can today be the day we slow it all down? Can today be the day we just enjoy being who and what we are? Can today be that day?

I hope so.

Take in this gift. Share it. Smile, laugh and enjoy each moment of each day.

Clear Your Mind by Clearing the Clutter

Clutter is a very potent inducer of stress. Clutter generates lots of sensory input. When we have too many sensory inputs, we have stress.

Arriving home to piles of newspapers and magazines just reminds us of an incomplete chore. It creates guilt because we have not read that stack of material. Plants need watering, tchotchkes need dusting, the list goes on and on.

I'm not saying we should trash our flowers (I love mine!) or that we should cancel our subscriptions and shove those papers into a drawer so we can ignore them.

What I am saying is that we can help ourselves by organizing and clearing the clutter. Doing so can help us enjoy a new sense of calm.

The task is to reduce our sensory overload; the more we can help ourselves create a clutterless environment, the easier it will be to reduce some stress.

Here are some ideas to help us clear up the clutter:

1. Start with a small amount of time. Ten minutes, maybe a half hour. Remember, stressing to find the time defeats the purpose of what we're trying to do.
2. Decide where you want to begin. Pick something small — a desktop, a coffee table, the fridge. Later, move on to a closet (one shelf at a time!), a room — and before you know it, you will have mastered the entire house!

3. Next, pull everything off the surface or out of the drawers. This lets us start with a clean slate.
4. Now examine each item and ask the following:
    – Do we need this?
    – Do we use it?
    – Have we used it in the past 12 months ?

If the answers are no — create four piles:

- Move it to another part of the house where it will be used
- Sell it
- Give it to a friend or charity
- Throw it away

It is important to choose one of the above for each item we have examined. Otherwise, the clutter just moves from room to room.

It is healthier for us when we can walk into a room with organized shelves and clear counters. Cutting down on the sensory input cuts down on our stress.

One *big* time-saver is putting like items in one place. All our tools or cleaning products should be together. We reduce stress by not having to search for an item all over the house.

We will feel lighter and calmer after we have created clutter-free spaces. Giving a new life to an unused item by giving or selling it will help us feel good.

Another tip to help clear the clutter: organize your time.

We all have a million things to do each week. As items come up, I write myself a note. Then on Sunday evenings (Ric does this late on Friday afternoons; you can find the time that works best for you) I assemble all my notes into one to-do list.

I make my list easier to complete by breaking things down into smaller tasks. If I need to call someone, I write down their phone number. If I need to drop someone a note, I address the envelope and put on a stamp so the letter is ready for me to write and mail. By getting these prep details out of the way, I can take my time focusing on the content.

By the time Monday arrives, I'm ready to start the week feeling relaxed, not stressed. Sure, I have lots to do, but I also have everything ready so I can do it at my leisure. With one list, I am ready for the week.

Getting organized frees our mind. We'll feel so good! We'll have time for more fun without feeling rushed! We'll be able to find time for things that make us happy.

Anything to reduce the stress and find some calm is so helpful. Have fun clearing the clutter!

Words of Wisdom

"Love the moment, and the energy of that moment will spread beyond all boundaries."

~Sister Corita Kent (1918-1986), artist/educator

Try It and See

Turn Down the Volume and Tune In...to Yourself

Did you know that all life has a measurable rate of electrical energy? Are you aware that stress, lack of sleep and illness all affect our health and therefore our electrical energy? When we go, go, go and give so much of ourselves, we are depleting our energy to the point where there is nothing left of us for us.

So, let's ask ourselves, "If we're tired and depleted of energy, what can we do to feel like ourselves again?"

Let's look at our day and see what we can bring awareness to and change:

- **TV**: loud and violent or fun and happy?
- **Food**: fresh or processed?
- **Daily interactions**: happy or not so happy?
- **Drive time**: nice music or the news?
- **Home**: finding enough downtime or rushing from one thing to the next?

Observing and being more aware can motivate us to make adjustments. Soon we will begin to feel better.

Let's make time to tune in to ourselves. We will find that small adjustments will bring wonderful results. We have the power to make ourselves healthier and happy.

Up in a Puff of Smoke

Maybe I've had a run of bad luck, but I have found myself interacting with a string of people who have been short tempered and grumpy. Sound familiar?

Instead of responding in kind, I do my best to bring on a BIG smile. To help me keep smiling when someone is rude, I make it a habit to never leave the house without my "Happy Armor."

Happy is a decision we make upon waking each day. Armor is how we keep the happy going when we are faced with difficult situations or difficult people. So, let's start with the decision to be happy.

To help build our Happy Armor, let's ask ourselves some questions: What bothers us? What worries us? Are there any old emotions or feelings we are not able to let go of? For one week, let's carry a pen and paper with us, and every time we feel like answering one of those questions or come upon a stressful situation, or when we wake up in the middle of the night worrying about something, write it down. Fold up each sheet of paper, and stash them in a bowl. Hide the bowl from our family; these papers are ours alone to see.

At the end of the week, take that bowl of worries, feelings and troubles outside. Find a vessel in which we can safely build a fire, such as a grill, hibachi or fire pit. Take a deep breath and put a match to them. As the pages burn, say, "Good-bye, worries."

Let go, let go, let go…of those worries and concerns. In trying this exercise, observe the days that follow; notice how some things have changed. We might make some wonderful discoveries. We might find it easier to wake up happy, and it will be easier to stay happy. This exercise will help us realize that we hold onto too much. We can do this exercise as many times as we want. When we begin to feel bogged down, simply write and burn.

By clearing away our stale emotions and worries, we create a better suit of armor. By clearing away the old we can take in more of the love and compliments from those around us. Then when you encounter a difficult situation or person, just keep smiling as it all bounces off our armor.

Not all days are easy and wonderful. We need to take care of ourselves, so burn away the worries, build up our armor and we will find our happy!

Try It and See

Carry around your pen and paper for a week. Write down items as they occur. Collect them, and at the end of the week burn them. See how your next week feels!

Words of Wisdom

"Be done with knowing and your worries will disappear."

~*The Tao Te Ching of Lao Tzu*, sage of the 6th century B.C.

Catch the Wave

We walk into a room and immediately get a sense of the mood. What was our clue?

Academic studies show that emotions are like germs — easily transmittable. Humans tend to mimic another person's body language and facial expressions.

Commenting on the results of one study, John T. Cacioppo, a psychology professor and director of the Center for Cognitive and Social Neuroscience at the University of Chicago, says, "The muscle fibers [in your face and body] can be activated unbeknownst to us."

We need to be aware of the mechanics of reading people, because understanding body language reveals the nonverbal communication that is occurring, enabling us to choose whether we want to join the conversation or not. If it's negative, we can simply walk away. Just having the awareness gives us choices.

This also explains why we should enter every situation with a smile on our face. We'll transmit it to everyone who's present. Talk about changing the world around us! All it takes to feel good is to smile. Our brain will do the rest!

Paul Ekman, emeritus professor of psychology at the University of California, San Francisco, has discovered that there is a connection between emotions and expressions. He says, "If we make a facial expression voluntarily, we can change the autonomic and central nervous system to generate that emotion." So instead of saying that we smile when we're happy, just smile and we'll become happy!

The key is to make sure we are transmitting the positive emotion. We might not be able to be smiling and positive all the time, but if we can be sure to smile when interacting with others, it is a start.

Remember: we transmit our mood to those around us. Our vibrations affect other people, so choose to make a difference. Find the positive in everything around us. Send out those smiles. We'll all be better for it.

Try It and See

How do we keep that smile going?

1. Stop and take a moment before we speak. Put on a smile before we open our mouth.
2. Before entering a room or stepping into the house, take a few deep breaths and turn on the smile.
3. Try yoga or meditation. The quiet moments can help us become more naturally positive and easygoing.
4. Take walks during our day. Breathe deeply and swing our arms as we walk. We'll find it's impossible to frown while we do this.
5. Have the courage to walk away from situations or people who bring us down.
6. Sing — turn up the music and have a good ol' time.
7. Dance — let our favorite music guide our movements as we move.

Words of Wisdom

"A warm smile is the universal language of kindness."

~William Arthur Ward (1921-1994), author

Wake Up to Time

Roman Emperor Marcus Aurelius (90-121 A.D.) said, "Time is a sort of river of passing events, and strong is its current."

We are surrounded by clocks. They're everywhere — on our cell phones, tablets and computers; in our cars; displayed on microwave ovens; even on our televisions and radios. And of course, on our wrists.

We live lives that are scheduled to the minute. We complain that we don't have enough time. We buy books and hire consultants to help us manage it. But do we really understand the essence of time?

As Aurelius said, time is a river that flows on relentlessly. Each minute that passes is irreplaceable. The days, weeks and months pass so quickly, they become a blur. We are so impatient to get to the *next* thing, we waste the now, the here, the present.

On a recent evening, I enjoyed visiting a good friend along with her mom and sister. We had coffee. We talked about life, family, food, crocheting and a myriad of other topics. There was no place else I wanted to be but with these wonderful women. Yes, there were 10 other things I needed to do, but it was pure joy to push it all out of my mind and sit and talk.

My wish for everyone is to find a way to be in the now. Appreciate the task at hand, the people in our life. Each moment is precious; once it is gone, we can't have it back.

Wake up to time! By being aware of the progression of time, we'll be motivated to make better choices in our day. Begin each day spending a few moments thinking about how we can best use our time.

It takes practice to live in the moment, to be awake to time. So let me offer these ideas that may help.

Focus on one thing at a time. It is very hard to do this. Practice — start out small. Our nature is to multitask throughout our day. But try it; pick anything — grocery shopping, grading papers, sitting at a soccer game, playing with your children. Just push all other thoughts away and focus on one thing. It will be like a mini-vacation packed into a few short minutes.

Enjoy the people in our life. We've all lost family and friends. We are blessed to have been able to share time with them. Losses make us acutely aware of time, how precious it is, how quickly it flows, how we can't ever get it back.

Wake up to time. Focus on the now. Enjoy the people in your life. Embrace the moments.

Try It and See

While you are in the quiet start of your day, stop and prioritize your activities. Can anything be moved, delayed or deleted?

Words of Wisdom

"Lost time is never found again."

~ Benjamin Franklin (1706-1790), Founding Father

Is Your Brain Asking for a Time-Out?

Do we find ourselves snapping at others, not sleeping through the night, feeling unsettled, being unable to focus or having a hard time remembering things? These could be signs that your brain is asking for a time-out.

For many of us, daily life seems a bit out of control. We let our commitments keep us from finding time for ourselves.

The National Center for Complementary and Alternative Medicine, part of the National Institutes of Health, offers 25 years of research that show how the relaxation response to meditation can help us gain the time-out our brain needs. Studies show that we can enjoy:

- increased production of the calming hormones melatonin and serotonin
- decreased production of the stress hormone cortisol
- increased immune factors
- increased youth-related hormone DHEA
- calmer brain-wave activity

All these factors are beneficial for several hours after meditation ends. It's hard to find that quiet time or time-out, but if we can, it will do wonders for our general health.

The book *Meditation as Medicine* by Dharma Singh Khalsa, MD, and Cameron Stauth shows that the benefits increase the longer we meditate:

- **3 minutes** — increased blood circulation begins, distributing enhanced neuroendocrine secretions throughout the body
- **7 minutes** — brain patterns begin to shift from static beta waves to calmer alpha waves and ultimately to deep-relaxation delta waves
- **11 minutes** — the sympathetic and parasympathetic nervous systems begin to accommodate increased energy
- **22 minutes** — anxiety-producing thoughts in the subconscious begin to clear
- **31 minutes** — endocrinologic balance is achieved, and this persists throughout the day, reflected by changes in mood and behavior.

Some friends have told me that when they sit for 30 minutes doing nothing, so many thoughts keep coming into their minds. Yes, that is normal. The key is to let those thoughts pass; don't hold onto them. Let them keep coming until there are no more. Then we will get to the good stuff, the real quiet time. The more we practice, the easier we will find reaching the quiet stage.

We need to take care of ourselves. We can start by giving our brain a time-out.

Go Online

Any action done with awareness is meditation. Meditation means being fully aware of our actions, thoughts, feelings and emotions. Another name for meditation is passive awareness.

To learn more about research related to meditation, go to:

www.nccam.nih.gov/research
(once in the website, search for "meditation")

www.mayoclinic.com (search for "meditation")

www.meditationworkshop.org

Summer State of Mind

What is it about summer that makes us feel lighter and carefree? We are more relaxed and inclined to act spontaneously — heading to the movies and dinner, and gathering with family and friends.

For those who planned and saved, your relaxed state is probably due to the fact that you worked so hard over the winter months to put plans into place so that you can now head to the shore, mountains, lakes and rivers. There is great tradition and ritual in vacations. We go to our favorite places and spend time with our favorite people, enjoying our favorite summertime foods and drinks.

The smells, tastes and feelings we experience while at our favorite vacation place help each of us become a different person, reliving our youth, willing (though perhaps not as often as in years before!) to take on a little adventure. With great anticipation, we embark on the road that will take us to our destination.

But where is it written that we must travel to gain that Summer State of Mind? Summers at home can be just as exciting! There is real fun in being outdoors, gardening, grilling, walking, biking and completing all the items on our to-do list that have been building up since the first part of the year. Summer downtime easily translates into personal time, giving us a most welcome chance to take a break, refocus and catch up.

Try It and See

While we are doing all this, here are some activities that are sure to cause us to smile. Forget the kids — these ideas are perfect for adults!

- Create finger paintings and spin art.

- Make your favorite ice pop by freezing your favorite fruit juice.

- Sleep in a tent in the backyard.

- Plan an entire day to do nothing.

- Play hopscotch and four square.

- Walk around all day with a camera and take lots of photos.

- Get out the music you grew up with and dance by the light of the moon.

- Have an ice cream party.

- Organize a game of flashlight tag or kick the can.

- Catch fireflies.

- Build a campfire and roast marshmallows.

- Visit a museum you've always wanted to explore.

- See some movies on your list.

- Sit outside and sip a glass of lemonade.

Let our Summer State of Mind help us recharge, regroup and unwind no matter where we are, who we are with or what our activity.

The Beginner's Mind

Beginners believe there are many possibilities. Experts believe there are few.

The beginner's mind is innocent of preconceptions, expectations, judgments and prejudices. It is a mind that does not approach things with a fixed point of view or prior judgment.

Yet in our daily lives we tend to approach tasks with a "been there, done that" mentality. We have lost the beginner's mind, the innocence of looking at something for the first time. We have lost the curiosity and the desire to learn more.

Carrying a lifetime of judgment and prejudices takes a lot of effort and mental energy. Although our past experiences can help us deal with new experiences, in many cases our minds are closed to new experiences.

Think about it this way. We walk into a situation that we have experienced many times before. It has gone badly in the past and we *know* it will go badly this time. We are tense, holding our breath, gripping our hands, our shoulders stiff. Wow, do we even realize how much strength and energy are being used for all that?

Let's stop and observe ourselves. Can we see that we have a pre-judged mind that is telling us how it is going to be? I don't know about you, but I don't like anyone telling me how it is going to be (not even my own mind). I like to explore and decide for myself.

Here's a cute example of the "expert's mind." My niece and nephews visit us often. Ric and I feel it is important to challenge them and expose them to new things. So when they announced that they wanted to watch a DVD one evening, we suggested a movie we knew they'd never seen: *Arsenic and Old Lace*. But my nephew loudly declared that he wanted to watch ONLY a movie he had seen before, because he KNEW he would like it. He was demonstrating an "expert" mind — closed to anything new.

We see this often in ourselves: we enter a situation with a mind-set of "I know" or "I've done that before." Without the balancing of the beginner's mind, we will miss anything new that may be out there waiting for us. But there is always something new we can learn or observe.

So, let's start again. Let's try the beginner's mind. We walk into a familiar situation. We push those old thoughts out and start breathing. We swing our arms freely, and we're smiling. Consider it a game, one where we win by finding something new and fun. Maybe we'll find something new or interesting from a person in the group. It could be anything. The fun part is finding it.

Yes, we have jobs, schedules and busy, busy lives. But if we can, start the day with a beginner's mind. Play the game to find the new. Find the fun. Find the beauty. It is a game we'll be glad we played.

It is not easy to always have the beginner's mind. We can be quick to slip back into old patterns of thinking. Try it, you'll like it. It might be for only 10 seconds the first time, but don't give up. We may find it fun to keep this beginner's mind around. We can turn it on and off as we need. When we turn out the lights to end our day, I believe we will have some smiles when we think about the fun new things we experienced.

Words of Wisdom

"The beginner's mind: openness, eagerness and the lack of pre-conceptions when approaching every aspect of life."

~ Shunryu Suzuki, author of *Zen Mind, Beginner's Mind* (1904-1971), monk/teacher

What I'd Have Said at Commencement

It was May, and Ric and I were on the podium for commencement at Rowan University. It's our alma mater, where we met 34 years ago. (Yikes, I'm not that old. Anyway…)

As the speeches progressed, I was glad I wasn't speaking, but I began to compose my own message to the new graduates.

I began to reflect on the path Ric and I took.

We were never spenders. Soon after we married, we became burdened with medical bills. I needed surgery. We were new to the workforce, our insurance did not cover much and we ended up with some big bills. Add in my school loans, and we quickly began the effort to figure out how to "eat this elephant" that was now living with us. The answer, we realized, was to take one bite at a time.

So we got started. We were not afraid to go without. Each and every spending decision we examined closely. Did we need this item or expense? Or did we merely want it? If it was a want, we would say no. We could not afford luxuries while we were busy paying off debts.

To raise cash, we sold most of our possessions, including our television. It would be four years before we'd buy another. Trust me, when you sell all your possessions in a yard sale to pay your bills, you are forever cured of materialism. Materialism is pointless. It's just stuff. Life is not about the stuff. Stuff is replaceable. Clothes, furniture, televisions — it can all be replaced.

Denying ourselves "luxury" items taught us a lot. We learned we could wait. Waiting led to the discovery of anticipation, which is a fun feeling. Anticipation creates motivation, which got us to work harder and not tire while we were working our second or third job.

We also found it important to constantly stay focused on our goals. When you are young and newly married, there are pages of things you want in your life. We would tour model homes and test-drive fancy cars and envision the day when we could own them. We would dream and keep our focus on our future.

We'd do little things because we couldn't do big ones. One trick, which we still do today, is to spend only dollar bills, never the coins. When we receive change back, we keep it. The change goes into an old peanut can that Ric still has. At the end of the month we roll up the coins and are amazed to find $30 or $40 that goes toward paying another bill.

I know today is different. People pay $5 for a latte and in New York $13.50 for a pack of cigarettes. But when you are young and in your late teens and early 20s — well, any age, for that matter — these small purchases add up and affect your financial future. Ric and I were disciplined and did not spend on small items. We are not special. You just have to be willing to sacrifice a little now for big rewards later. I'd tell the graduates to live within their means, spend less than they earn and save a little. They'll be a lot better off.

We didn't own a credit card until we were in our mid-30s. We paid cash for everything. If we did not have the cash, we did not buy it. ATM? We've never used one. We would get cash from the bank on Friday, and if we ran out of cash during the weekend, we stopped spending. No plastic meant no way for us to spend more than was prudent.

Commencement day speeches are all about hope and the future. I would love to give graduates a message that weaves in a little prag-matism, too.

Maybe next year.

Back to the Farm

We have one body, and we need to take care of it. Let's get more specific to say we have one *immune system,* and we need to take care of it.

Over the past several decades, there has been a tremendous increase in the number of autoimmune diseases — why?

One theory says we are too clean. This "hygiene hypothesis" suggests that we have created such a clean society that our immune systems have fewer command-and-control cells known as regulatory T cells. We need lots of these for a healthy immune system. This is especially important for the young; they need to be exposed to more of these cells as they grow so their immune systems will be strong.

To combat this problem, some scientists suggest we "get back to the farm." By exposing ourselves regularly to grasses, animals and dirt, our bodies can build immunities. Long gone are the days when kids played outside, finding adventures in the dirt and sloshing through streams. No one just hangs out in the fields, looking as clouds float by and imagining shapes. Today, kids' time is much more structured and electronic oriented.

The price for our "progress" is a compromised immune system. It renders us more susceptible to disease, especially when we add stress.

Here are some suggestions to help with a healthy immune system:

1. **Breathe** — Normal breathing is shallow. What we want is to become more aware of our breath and take deep breaths. We

want relaxed abdominal breathing. This calms the immune system.

2. **Eat small meals** — It is very stressful for our bodies to process food. There is a lot going on with each swallow. Try eating four to six small meals during the day. Add healthy snacks between our main meals, and eat smaller amounts at breakfast, lunch and dinner. The Hobbits were right: breakfast, second breakfast, elevenses, lunch, afternoon tea, supper, dinner — that's the way to go.

3. **Get high-quality sleep** — This is a toughie! Listen to music, use some lavender oil, turn off the television. Create a ritual that brings us to a relaxed state so we can sleep more deeply.

4. **Incorporate rhythmic activities into your day** — Try dancing, swimming, rowing or walking to music. The rhythmic exercise synchronizes with the natural rhythms of our heartbeat and breathing.

5. **Stay connected** — The bonds we have with our spouse, children, friends and pets help keep away anxiety and depression. When we are feeling down, reach out and contact someone we have not talked to in a while.

6. **Create a soothing environment** — Our immune systems do not like noise and chaotic environments. They prefer to be outside; they prefer an environment that is calm.

7. **Eat well** — Stay away from processed foods. Eat fresh foods whenever possible. Find a reputable nutritionist who can help make sure we are getting the proper nutrients and eating a varied diet.

We have only one immune system. We need to take care of it. It is the core of our health. Get outside more. Take in each day with joy and love, for tomorrow is not guaranteed.

Go Online

To learn more, visit:
science.howstuffworks.com
www.kidshealth.org
www.niaid.nih.gov/topics/immunesystem

Are You Listening to Your Own Nonverbal Communication?

We all know how easy it is to communicate without words. All it takes is a glance, a raised eyebrow or a frown. But are we listening to the quiet voice inside?

I'm talking about instinct and intuition. Researchers at the University of Hawaii and the National Institutes of Health, who have been studying nonverbal communication since the 1960s, describe the importance of being aware of who and what is around. In an article published by *National Geographic Adventure,* they talked about being on vacation and trusting strangers and unfamiliar surroundings.

On a conscious level we are taking in the sights, but it is our subconscious that is taking in the smaller details and developing a conclusion. This is what we need to pay attention to.

When it comes to body language, are we leaning in (we like or agree) or leaning out (we dislike or disagree)? Crossing our arms is a sign of discomfort, and placing our hands on our hips is an act of dominance. Fussing with hair or jewelry reflects emotional discomfort, doubt or insecurity; ditto for constant leg motion. However, crossed legs or toes pointing up means we're comfortable or in a positive mood.

When our intuition is trying to communicate with us, we will feel different sensations — our stomach might tighten, we might feel tingling or the hair on the back of our neck will react. We need to listen so we can act — walk away from a situation, tell a person we're with that we're not feeling right about what's happening. Our instinct/intuition is always active; we need to tune in as often as possible. It is hard to do when we're playing with our electronics, so put them down and pay attention to what is going on around us. We'll be safer.

Trust that inner voice. Believe in ourselves. Don't get lost in technology. It is not a replacement for our instinct and intuition.

Have fun by stopping for a moment each day to see what our instinct and intuition are telling us. We'll become more in tune with ourselves and with the world around us.

Words of Wisdom

"Learn to get in touch with silence within yourself and know that everything in this life has a purpose. There are no mistakes, no coincidences; all events are blessings given to us to learn from. There is no need to go to India or anywhere else to find peace. You will find that deep place of silence right in your room, your garden or even your bathtub."

~Elisabeth Kubler-Ross (1926-2004), Swiss-American psychiatrist

"Built into you is an internal guidance system that shows you the way home. All you need to do is heed the voice."

~ Neale Donald Walsch, author

Hanging Out the Wash

One of our many family gatherings happened to be in Cape May, N.J., where we rented an old Victorian house. Upon arrival, everyone wandered around, exploring what was their home for the next week. Out back, we all noticed two poles with a rope strung between them. Well, this was very strange to my niece and nephew, who had never seen such a thing. I laughed because I could not believe they had never seen a clothesline.

Growing up, we always had a clothesline. It was a fun task to hang all the clothes in the nice warm sun. Well, reengaging in this activity of the past proved to be one of the most relaxing aspects of the vacation.

It is amazing to watch a family come together. In our case, four households converged. I found myself sitting back and observing the rhythm that developed. It began in the kitchen and the laundry room. The clothes washer ran nonstop, emitting a steady, calming, almost hypnotizing sound as the clothes went round and round. This clothesline added another experience as we took the laundry outside to dry.

I fear that many have never seen — or even heard of — a clothesline. (And if you have, thanks for commiserating.) As I grew up, we did not have a clothes dryer until I was eight years old. Even then, my mother used it only for towels; everything else went out on the line.

I remember that line fondly, and our summer in Cape May brought back the same warm feelings.

Hanging clothes out to dry is surprisingly relaxing. You get to enjoy the fresh air and the sun's warmth while tending to each piece of clothing one by one. The task can't be rushed, so there's no attempt to do so. Figuring out how to fit all the clothes onto the line was a fun puzzle to solve. And when finished, watching the clothes sway gently in the breeze was calming.

So even though life is now fast and there is no time to hang clothes outside to dry, we can dream and embrace the concept: we need simply to slow down. Here are some ways we can:

- If we are hosting family, make time to sit back and notice the rhythms that emerge as everyone spends time together.
- Find a project with a beginning, a middle and an end. There is great satisfaction in having something to show for our time.
- Take a moment to look around. Pay attention to all the life, people and things around us. There is so much we miss each day because we are moving too fast. Slow down and try to discover one new thing each day. We'll be surprised at what we notice.
- Make our time count. Try to fill our moments with people and projects that are meaningful to us. When we can define what is most important to us, it is easier to say no when we need to.
- Find a project that will reconnect us to the outdoors. For some wonderful reason, everything naturally slows down when we are out walking or gardening.

After our family gathering, I knew I wanted to share my experience of hanging out the wash. Later, while shopping with my sister, I came upon a book titled *Hanging Out the Wash and Other Ways to Find More in Less* by Adair Lara. Funny what people write about.

I hope you find your clothesline.

Let's Get Happy

We are all drawn to drama. Between life and the TV there is an endless supply. The Nielsen Company says we watch 151 hours of television per month. For more than five hours a day we're barraged by negativity. Watching television dramas is unsettling because the shows depict perfect people living perfect lives in perfect homes, while commercials show big problems being solved in just 30 seconds — and we wonder why we can't keep up!

Because we can't control the images that the television throws at us, we need to take control. We control ourselves, our attitudes and our actions. We control our happiness. This is easier for us to do by turning off the television and changing the way we look at the world.

Let's find some happiness. Gaze at the beautiful blue sky and realize that we have this moment, this day, to find the good and the happy. There are small miracles happening around us all the time — we need only to look around to see them.

It is time to take positive steps to take back our happy. By making do with less, we begin to take control. By realizing that we don't have to keep up with the proverbial Joneses and focusing in on what is real and what is important, we will get a better sense of self. Simple is in.

Start a little happy list. Here are some ideas I came up with:

- Hosting family game and movie nights
- Giving and getting hugs from the little ones
- Walking the dogs and watching them enjoy the day
- Enjoying a big ice cream cone on a warm day
- Baking a cake instead of buying one
- Flowers
- Music
- Laughter

This is our finest hour. Let's turn off the television and tune in to the things that matter. Embrace the change, spin the positive and see what happens.

Words of Wisdom

"There has not been a single day since the world began when the sun was not shining. The trouble has been with our vision."

~Anonymous

Go Online

To learn more, visit:
www.psychologytoday.com/basics/happiness
www.authentichappiness.sas.upenn.edu

Love to Laugh

We love to laugh. Want to know why?

Physiologically speaking, laughter is the activation of the ventrome-dial prefrontal cortex, which sends endorphins to the body. These endorphins are *great* for us. They strengthen our immune system, boost our energy, diminish pain and protect our heart from stress. They help us through difficult times when problems seem over-whelming.

This is why it's important that we have laughter in our lives every day. Laughing connects us to others and helps us improve our per-spective.

Laughter is contagious. It affects our immediate social circle, and as a 20-year study of 5,000 people conducted by Harvard Medical School and the University of California, San Diego, discovered, the impact of laughter lasts up to one year and can create a "smile chain reaction" that continues far beyond the people we know.

It's also vital that we laugh at ourselves. Life is constantly throwing challenges our way. It is easy to get down or to take ourselves or our situation too seriously. So the next time we are given a problem, play with it as though the problem were a toy. Learn to laugh at ourselves by asking these questions:

- Is the problem really worth getting upset over?
- Is it worth upsetting others?
- Is it really so irreparable?
- Is it really our problem, or does it belong to someone else?

Sometimes problems really are worth the angst they cause, but often we'll discover that the issue is actually something that instead deserves nothing more than laughter.

So let's keep a sense of humor and find laughter somewhere in our day. Stepping back helps. Pause to laugh at our situation. Laughter helps us keep a positive, optimistic outlook during difficult moments, and there is nothing that works faster to bring the body back into balance than a good laugh. Laughter lightens our burdens, inspires hope, connects us to others, and keeps us grounded and focused.

How do we start?

By smiling. Then:

- Count your blessings — make a list of all the good in your life.
- Spend time with fun people.
- Watch a funny movie.
- Find something silly to do — have a pillow or water fight.
- Play with the kids or pet.
- Roll around on the ground and forget all the rules.
- Join with others to set aside a five-minute "laugh out loud" break. Even do this at work!

The fact is, we absorb the frequency, environment and mood around us. These stay with us and we pass them to others. So let's laugh and pass it on.

Laugh and pass it on. ☺

Words of Wisdom

"To affect the quality of the day; that is the art of life."

~Henry David Thoreau (1817-1862), American author, poet and philosopher

Acceptance

The world around us is constantly changing. Nothing, it seems, is as it was. Rather than dwell on how things were, it is healthier to accept our lives as they are now. That means accepting ourselves as well and accepting others, too, just as they are.

When we accept, we no longer hold onto baggage. Acceptance helps us become more patient, forgiving and relaxed. We can be gentle with ourselves and others. This is our greatest peace.

Without acceptance we will not be able to move into the change that is coming. Yes, I lost my job; yes, I lost my house; yes, my kids are in different schools; no, I can't retire this year; the list can go on.

Taking a stance of acceptance allows us to say, "Okay, I'm in a different living environment; okay, I have an opportunity to find different work; okay, my kids get to experience new friends; okay, I get to hang out longer with the folks at work." Look at acceptance as water washing over us instead of pounding us into the rocks.

Acceptance gives us a sense of freedom. If we can accept ourselves just as we are with all our faults and all the mistakes we've made along the way, we can stop beating ourselves up. Acceptance lets us be okay with who we are.

Acceptance of others can remove a great weight from our shoulders. When we don't have to work so hard at changing someone, wow, we can now relax and enjoy the moment with them. Okay, people can annoy us, but accepting them as they are and rolling with the moment make life a whole lot easier.

Accept our life right now, just as it is. The lessons and obstacles along the way have enriched the moment we are in now. Breathe it all in and enjoy where we are.

Try It and See

Acceptance can be hard work. So let's try a little exercise to help us give away the things we hold onto that make acceptance so difficult.

Self: Create a list of all the things we are critical of about ourselves that we can't seem to move past.

Others: Create a list of those in our immediate life and the aspects about them we tend to criticize.

Life: Create a list of what bothers us.

Let's take these lists and burn them. (In a safe place, please!) As we watch these lists burn, we let go of bonds they have on us. As we watch the lists burn, let us bring in acceptance of who we are and of the others in our lives. Let us restore our peace and balance through acceptance.

Words of Wisdom

"When we get too caught up in the busyness of the world, we lose connection with one another — and ourselves."

~Jack Kornfield, Buddhist monk, teacher of meditation

"Acceptance and tolerance and forgiveness, those are life altering lessons."

~Jessica Lange, actress

Listening to Your Inner Voice

On one of our business trips, Ric and I were done with our meetings and on our way to enjoy the evening with friends.

On our way to dinner, our taxi was hit by another car. Thankfully everyone was fine, and within the hour we were enjoying a glass of wine with our colleagues.

But a comment Ric made at the scene of the accident got my attention. As we were standing around, waiting to talk to the police officer, Ric turned to me and said, "I knew something bad was going to happen in that cab. I had a bad feeling as we were walking out of the hotel."

I turned to him and asked him why he didn't listen to that voice, that feeling he had. Why didn't he do what it was telling him? In this case it was telling him not to get into that cab.

This may sound silly. But we do get messages — and we need to listen to them. If we can slow down enough to listen we would realize we get them throughout the day. Call this person. Drop so-and-so a note. Cancel this until another day.

To hear our inner voice, we need to slow down enough and turn inward. When we are open to our intuition we can get a better sense of the proper direction to take. We can learn our truth and rise above fear and ego, which keep us blocked in.

Our inner voice (intuition) comes from our head, our heart and our gut. How do we recognize it? We recognize it as a quiet yet firm voice. Or it can feel like someone is tugging at our heart or our stomach. It can feel like a tap on the shoulder or be something visual (for example, we might see a specific symbol or word multiple times throughout the day). These are quiet little messages that are trying to get our attention.

It can take time to learn how to hear our intuition/inner voice. At first, it may not seem clear. We don't trust what we are hearing. Or we may not understand what is being said. Only later — after our accident, in Ric's case — do we realize we had ignored the message.

We begin our day listening to the news, to our spouse or to our kids. What if we began our day listening to ourselves? Wow, that would be a good day!

Notes to Notice

By listening, we can validate our experiences and look forward to our next message. Another opportunity will come soon enough — and if we follow our intuitive voice and if we learn to stay true to it, we become empowered. We are not conforming to someone else's opinion of who we should be. It is all about being true to ourselves and all the good that comes from that. It's about the freedom to move about in our own personal truth.

Words of Wisdom

"The more you trust your intuition, the more empowered you become, the stronger you become and the happier you become."

~Gisele Bundchen, model

"The only real valuable thing is intuition."

~Albert Einstein (1879-1955), father of modern physics

Finding Joy in the little Things

A new companion for our dog, Summer, is Vicki. We've enjoyed observing and getting to know Vicki. The most fun is watching her start her day.

Out of respect, I always open Summer's crate first each morning. While she is clearly happy to see me, each morning I find her all curled up in her bed, looking at me with an expression of, "Do I have to get up?"

Vicki, though, is different. She sits up alertly waiting for me, tail wagging furiously. When I open her crate she jumps out, goes immediately to her basket of toys and grabs one with great gusto, tail wagging fast. Off she trots to begin her day, toy in mouth. She picks a different toy each day, and no matter which one she selects, that toy is the greatest thing in the world to her at that moment.

The excitement of that start continues throughout each day, which she fills with adventure — chasing small creatures, running for the fun of it and playing with her new sister.

Vicki is bringing a new light into our lives. She wakes each day with a light heart, not just ready for any small adventure that might come her way and not just actively looking for one, but fully expecting to find one.

And she is never disappointed! She starts her day truly happy! The dog has no baggage, no judgments. She begins each day with a clean canvas on which to paint — and her toy basket is filled with brushes.

Vicki is teaching us how to find joy. She shows us that joy can come in little things and that the source of joy can change from moment to moment. Joy is just around the corner and waiting to be found.

Vicki is even helping Summer find joy and release some of her fears. When Vicki takes a toy or bone, she does so with great joy, love and playfulness. At first, this took Summer by surprise. I could see that she was nervous, not sure how Vicki would act. But Summer's mind has been opened to change, and she has seen Vicki's joy, love and playfulness in everything she does. Now Summer's fears, like an onion, are peeling away, and she's beginning to relax and become more playful and happy, too.

We all have patterns ingrained in us by our past. Sometimes those patterns are negative or even hurtful. But if we can break those patterns, we can find happiness and joy.

Fear is one of those big patterns. If we have a lot of fear in our lives, it might be helpful to make a list of what makes us fearful. Then, like Summer, release them.

It takes time and sometimes encouragement from others, as Summer is learning from Vicki. And I know that one day soon, Summer will wake as Vicki does: tail wagging and with great joy and gusto to begin anew.

Let's discard our fears, grab our toy and start our day!

Try It and See

List 3 fears you have. Find a safe vessel and burn the list. Give yourself permission to release your fears.

List 3 joyful moments you find in your day.

_____   _____

_____   _____

_____   _____

The Other Side of the Story

One of the biggest hits on Broadway is the musical *Wicked,* based on the best-selling book by Gregory Maguire. The story is the prelude to *The Wizard of Oz* — the story we all grew up with and know so well. *Wicked* beautifully illustrates that there is always another view to the world we know.

Having had the chance to see the different side of the Wicked Witch made me think about times in my own life when I was not open to the other side of the story.

We get bombarded with stories every day from the media, our family and friends. It's so easy to get sucked into the version that we are told. This is especially true with family — so much emotion comes with each story that we are certain that what they're telling us must be true, and so we make their story our own.

Still, it is a bit scary when we accept stories as they are first presented and never ask questions — to never be open to the fact that there might be another side of the story. When did we lose that childhood trait of always (to every parent's dismay) asking questions?

When we refuse to consider that there might be other points of view or other versions of events, we become rigid. So many relationships are harmed because we are not open to other possibilities.

Our minds can be like trapdoors that always slam shut. It takes time and some stamina to be open to what can be. It can also be tremendous fun to each day look for what can be. We cannot accept everything at face value. There is more to the story, and we must commit ourselves to finding out what that is.

Here is a good exercise: start each day with the awareness of keeping an open mind. As we catch ourselves doing the opposite, let's try to listen to whatever is going on at the moment.

If we can make this small mental shift to what can be, we will be exposed to many wonderful things that were never before on our radar. We must pay attention to how many times in a day we shut out input from others because it is not what we know and because we are uncomfortable pondering the possibilities.

I saw a bumper sticker the other day that said "Don't believe what our mind tells us." This is great because it reminds us to question everything, to be open to all possibilities.

Have fun with our day. Open up, and let the wonders of the world find us.

Try It and See

Next time you encounter a person or situation that you are having trouble with, try this:

Stop — take a breath and pretend it is the first time you are meeting this person or engaging in the situation. If we can shift our thinking just a bit and experience the person or situation in a new way, it gives us a chance to start over. We get a chance to leave behind the old baggage and experience the person or situation at a different level.

Try it and you will be surprised by how the relationship changes — all for the better!

Words of Wisdom

"We need to teach the next generation of children from day one that they are responsible for their lives. Mankind's greatest gift, also its greatest curse, is that we have free choice. We can make our choices built from love or from fear."

~Elisabeth Kubler-Ross (1926-2004), Swiss-American psychiatrist

The Power We Give Words

I saw a cute movie the other day called *Penelope*. I won't spoil it for you, but will say that it conveys an important message: it is not the power of words but the power we give words.

We learn at a very early age the power of our words. The first word that babies all over the world say is often some version of "mom," and we quickly learn the benefits of saying it — it brings to us a great smile and waves of love from the person taking care of us. We quickly learn that speaking a word creates a reaction.

As we began our social interactions, we all experimented with words. We would throw out words and look for reactions. Sometimes the words were mean and we would hurt the feelings of someone close to us. Nice words generated many rewards. Even to this day, I bet we can remember our experiments. Even today, we can remember the kind words of a teacher and how those words encouraged us to do well.

As adults we know how our words work. We use them to show love and encouragement. We also use them to hurt people and break them down.

We should think about the power of our words when we interact with each other. If we would simply breathe and take a moment to carefully choose what we are about to say, if we looked the person in the eyes and watched their reaction, we would have a lot of powerful moments in our day. This is a lesson Penelope learned. We can change our world around with words and the power we give them.

I love you. I appreciate you. You look wonderful. Great job. Thank you. These words immediately make us feel good. Speaking a person's name along with these wonderful words should be in our daily routine.

When we speak, let's remember to think about the impact of the words we are about to send out.

Try It and See

List chances in your day where you can use your words to encourage and/or improve a situation.

_____

_____

_____

Words of Wisdom

"Whatever words we utter should be chosen with care, for people will hear them and be influenced by them for good or evil."

~Siddhartha Gautama Buddha (563-483 B.C.)

"I expect to pass through this world but once. Any good therefore that I can do, or any kindness that I can show to any fellow creature, let me do it now. Let me not defer or neglect it, for I shall not pass this way again."

~William Penn (1644-1718), philanthropist and founder of
the Commonwealth of Pennsylvania

Courage

Courage is a word that constantly rambles around in my head. This time there just happened to be a program commemorating the anniversary of the 9/11 attacks. I was amazed at the stories from people who were in the buildings. Where did they find the courage to survive?

In researching courage, I discovered *physical* courage — finding great strength in the midst of fear, not giving in to a desire to give up or find an easier way. This is the courage of those 9/11 survivors — finding amazing strength deep within themselves to overcome the threat they faced. I wonder: Where did they find that courage? How did they overcome their fear? And most of all, I wonder if I would be able to summon such physical courage if faced with a similar situation. After all, physical courage is not something we can practice in our daily lives — or can we?

In reading more, I found a second component: *moral* courage. Those who display this quality trust their inner strength. They have integrity in all areas of their lives. Being true to ourselves and our roles, not compromising or yielding to the pressures of individuals or situations around us, is moral courage. It is the ability to stand in our own truth when no one around us does.

To have moral courage each day is daunting. Boundaries often are fuzzy, and social norms are constantly changing. If we look outward, taking cues from others, we might take the wrong path. It takes moral courage to say no and follow our own sense of right and wrong. It takes moral courage not to follow what is popular when you do so merely because it is popular.

As Shakespeare wrote, "To thine own self be true." This is moral courage. Let's define our boundaries, be aware of right and wrong, and stand ready to fend off manipulation and social pressures.

Many others, in many ways, show us their courage. We, too, have the capacity to be courageous.

We must stand in our truth, and we must have the courage to do so.

Try It and See

What is one thing you wish you had the courage to do? Write it down and post it on your bathroom mirror so you look at it all the time. Keep notes and be observant of the changes as they occur.

I wish I had the courage to:

_____

_____

_____

Words of Wisdom

"We don't see things as they are, we see them as we are."

~Anaïs Nin (1903-1977), diarist

"Kind words can be short and easy to speak but their echoes are endless."

~Mother Teresa (1910-1997), nun, Missionaries of Charity, Nobel Peace Prize winner

The Unscheduled Calendar

The beauty of being us is that each moment of each day we have the opportunity to change, grow, learn and open up to the intentions and attitudes that create our life.

Every moment of every day we are in control of how we feel. We can choose to be happy or we can choose darker emotions. In order to keep us on the happy side we need to take more control of our day.

I began to notice that my calendar was getting out of control. Or rather, it had taken control over me. I kept looking to see what I could do to get my days back. I did something scary that turned out to be brilliant, so I wanted to share it with you.

Keep breathing.

I know this may freak you out.

Here goes:

I completely emptied one entire week. I canceled everything. I mean everything — to the point that people were calling me to find out what was going on. But I was determined to get ahead of this thing. Sunday night came along, I opened my calendar and I saw nothing there. I kept breathing. I got a good night's sleep and woke up Monday a little nervous.

What did I learn?

One, the fact that we feel the need to be busy is a myth. Being busy for the sake of being busy is a waste of time. It wastes our focus and energy.

Two, we need to make room in our day for what truly needs to be there. I had projects that needed attention. I found the time to complete them in my unscheduled week.

In my unscheduled week, I got more things done than ever, and before I knew it, Friday was here. I felt good. I felt grounded and happy with my accomplishments for the week.

Now I keep an unscheduled calendar. I allow only the items that are truly important. I don't fill the time for the sake of filling the time. In fact, if I don't see a lot of blank space on my calendar, I start looking at what is there and I ask myself if I really need to be a part of it.

We always have the opportunity to fine-tune our focus. A survey from TD Ameritrade reported that the most common goals were to reduce stress and have more fun. One way to achieve both goals is to unschedule ourselves!

Try it and see how much fun you can have!

Try It and See

What are 3 things that you could cancel this month? Start by clearing out one day and see how it feels to have freedom to move around as you wish. Also see how it naturally fills with things that are maybe more fun or rewarding.

_____

_____

_____

We Don't Know What We've Lost Until It's Gone

Noise! We don't realize what a noisy day-to-day life we have until we get away from it. Ric and I had a chance to take a break. We found an island that had no cars. It was so quiet we could hear the grass moving in the breeze. We were surrounded by the most amazing quiet. It took a little time for us to get used to it. The silence made us realize how much noise affects our bodies, because the mere absence of noise created an amazing state of relaxation.

To get a little scientific here, noise is any unwanted sound. (As Ric asks me to point out, no, this does not refer to your spouse talking.)

Noise is measured in decibels (dB); a whisper is measured at 30 dB, a conversation between two people is 60 dB, shouting is 80 dB. Noise from 85 dB to 120 dB is painful to most ears. In 1972, Congress passed the Noise Control Act because noise pollution was found to have a direct impact on our health: elevated stress levels, anxiety, depression, insomnia, high blood pressure, panic attacks and more, including, of course, noise-induced deafness.

Noise has an impact on our environment. It affects the balance that naturally occurs with our plants and animals. Noise affects animal communication and damages their ability to navigate. In a balanced world, the "voice" of animals would be heard over human-made sounds.

Individually, we can't reduce the noise that cars and airplanes create. But we can act nonetheless. Our first step is to resensitize our hearing. We need to expose ourselves to extreme quiet to help us understand that when we're being bombarded with noise we expose ourselves to tension.

We need to lower the volume, turn off the radio and television, get those headphones out of our ears, and walk away from noisy environments.

Here's an exercise to try:

Sit comfortably, feet on the floor, hands comfortably in your lap. Turn your attention to your ears. What do you hear immediately around you? It might be the hum of a nearby computer or the air-conditioning system. Maybe it's a person talking nearby. Just observe.

Next, focus your hearing outside the room or building. What do you hear? Is that a dog barking or a lawn mower? Can you hear cars going by? Or birds singing? How many different birds can you hear? Focus on those sounds. Just observe.

Next, listen for more distant sounds. Are airplanes passing by? Once you catch a distant sound, focus on it for as long as you can. Sometimes what we're hearing is…nothing. And that is where we find our moments of quiet. The further out we can bring our hearing, the more relaxed we feel. Try it. Some days we may get only to the edges of the room we are in, while on other days we may reach much further. This exercise can be done anywhere, anytime.

And to sustain this relaxation, demand that radios and televisions nearby be turned down. Carry a set of earplugs to the movies and concerts.

This reawakening of our hearing can help us be a little healthier, reduce the stress a bit. Find some quiet. Once we get comfortable with it, we will crave it.

Try It and See

Practice distance listening. Keep notes and observe how you feel after each session. Observe how long the relaxation lasts.

Traffic Jam

Returning from a family vacation, one of the many topics of conversation was my nephew getting his driver's permit.

Everyone had words of wisdom for him. Not so much about driving technique but mostly a philosophical approach to driving. Be kind, respectful, cooperative, have patience. Patience was a big one.

I found all this quite curious. I started laughing to myself because I know my family members and their behind-the-wheel personalities. Their behavior is nothing like the words that were coming out of their mouths.

As adults we want to impart wisdom to the young folk as they reach important points in their lives. It's natural that we want to teach them how it should be, not how it is.

There is a lot of academic literature on the psychology of driving. Driving, after all, is really a study of us. The research breaks driving into three categories: affect (our feelings), cognition (how we think) and behavior (our actions). Are we aware of how our actions affect others?

Most of us just hop behind the wheel, not bothering to realize that we're bringing our emotions into the vehicle. Are we upset about something? Stress pushes our foot onto the gas pedal. We race down neighborhood streets while replaying in our minds some event that has upset us. We're focused on lots of things but not our driving.

Think about all the nonverbal communication that's involved with our failure to use turn signals, drive at safe speeds, accelerate through yellow lights and make right-hand turns from the left lane.

My hope is that new drivers regard driving as the ultimate cooperative activity. Our behavior speaks volumes about us. Do we let folks move into our lane or do we speed up to cut them off? Are we tailgating or is there plenty of room between the car in front of us? Do we wave a thank-you when someone lets us into traffic?

We are all connected to each other and never more so than when we are driving. So when we enter our cars, let's take a moment before we start moving. Take a breath. Focus on being in the car. Leave behind where we were and what was going on before we entered the car. Take in our surroundings, adjust the mirrors and seat so we feel like part of the car. Take another breath. Just "be" in the car for a moment. And as we ride, remember that encounters with other drivers are not personal challenges but simply part of being safe.

Let's regard time in our cars as our opportunity to be cooperative and kind. Let's try to be in one place at a time — in our car. We will find our stress will be lower and we'll be happier.

Oh, and safer, too.

Try It and See

Next time you step into the car,

Stop.

Check in just for a moment — breathe — four counts in — four counts out.

Put the phone away.

Practice doing one thing at a time — driving!

Bliss

I had the honor of visiting my friend just a few days after she gave birth to her little girl. I was transformed while holding this new little one. The peace within her, her contentment and the bliss on her face have stayed with me.

I think deep down we all crave such inner peace, contentment and bliss. I have learned that we cannot find it in a noisy, busy world, and we cannot wait for others to help us find it. Bliss must come from within us — and we must find quiet, unscheduled time to let us find it.

So where do we begin? Let's start by finding some quiet. Let's plan some unscheduled time in our day. If we look hard, we can find a few minutes to turn the world off. Take our morning tea into our closet if we have to. Close our office door and look out the window. Step away from electronics. Go outside for a walk, get some fresh air. If we look hard enough, we'll find pockets of time when we can be quiet.

In the beginning, quiet is a bit hard to enjoy. It takes practice for our minds to turn off and focus on one thing — like our breath. Then the harder part comes: looking within. I think most of us stay busy so we don't have to look at our true selves. We can run, but we can't hide. Our true inner selves will catch up with us.

We need the quiet to think, to process life. We need the quiet so that there is room and space to ask big questions: What makes us happy? Do we love what we do? What fills our hearts and souls? It could be something as simple as strumming a guitar. It could be walking the dog. It could be arranging flowers. It could be working in a soup kitchen or teaching in a third-world country. The beauty is that it is different for all of us.

Bliss — a state of profound satisfaction, happiness and joy — is a state of mind undisturbed by gain or loss. The bliss and inner peace we enjoyed when we were new to this world are still inside us. We got busy with life and lost touch, so we just need to acknowledge that it is there. In the quiet we can say hello — it's safe to come out now. Finding that bliss and contentment will be transformational.

Words of Wisdom

"Imagination is more important than knowledge. Knowledge is limited. Imagination encircles the world."

~Albert Einstein (1879-1955), father of modern physics

"Follow your bliss and the universe will open doors where there were only walls."

~Joseph Campbell (1904-1987), mythologist, writer, lecturer

Honey, I'm Home

We spend our days away from the ones we love — at work, at school, involved with friends and the community. So what happens at the end of the day when we get home?

Often we're tired, maybe hungry, with a need for quiet to unwind. We don't want even one more thing to be asked of us. Yet this is the most demanding time of the day. A meal needs to be pulled together, children need to be kept on time for activities or homework, and pets need love, attention and food. It is a "me" time of day for each of us — all at once.

How do we enter this time less centered on ourselves and ready to interact with those in the family in a positive, engaged manner?

It is easy to turn on the television and tune out while the rest of the house is in a whirlwind. Remember the movie *The Incredibles*? The family is having dinner, the kids are out of control, the baby crying, the doorbell ringing — and Dad just sitting there, oblivious to all as he reads the newspaper.

It's at this point that Helen (aka Elastigirl) screams to Bob (aka Mr. Incredible): "This would be a good time to engage!"

So how do we do that? How can we be sure to engage when we cross the threshold of home?

First, let's decompress on the way home. Review the day in our minds, make our "steering wheel speeches," saying aloud to no one but us all the things we wish we'd said earlier in the day to others — and complete our speeches before entering the house. That way, we can have smiles on our faces when we arrive and not "dump" or relive our day at the expense of our family.

Second, let's create closure from the workday. Before entering the house, compile a list of what we need to do tomorrow. We can then set our list aside and not have to think about it all night.

Third, let's grant everyone transition time when they enter the house. Let them shed their work or school clothes, put away their belongings and acclimate to the new environment. We're anxious to see them and ready to tell them all we have to say, but we need to give them some time — maybe 15 minutes is all they need — to shed the outside world and be in the home as mentally and emotionally as they are physically.

Fourth, let's practice listening. Be engaged with everyone in the house. Be present with the family. Pay attention to what is not being said as much as to what is. Ask questions that can lead to deeper answers.

None of us lives with Ozzie and Harriet, the Petries, the Cleavers, the Partridges or the Brady Bunch. But we can still come together at the end of our day and be as happy as they were.

Coming home gives us a time to share in the tasks that need to be done, time to share in preparing a meal, time to enjoy one another and talk on a deeper level. It is a time for laughter and learning and a time to rest and prepare for another day.

Every time we come home, instead of merely being there, let's really be *at home*.

Notes to Notice

- Decompress
- Create closure to the day
- Give transition time
- Practice active listening

Seeing the Patterns in Our Lives

I'm in my mid-50s, and I don't need to create drama in my world. But late last year something began to brew. I could feel it. Something was bubbling up. At first it was a small rumble — you know, bits of cranky spilling out. Then the rumble got bigger, and in the new year it finally blew. Wow, was it huge!

It was an old pattern of thought and behavior that showed up to tell me I had not really dealt with an old issue. It was a wake-up call to finally address something I'd long been scooting around.

Have you ever felt something brewing inside? Do you find yourself dealing with it multiple times? When we notice a pattern, thought or unwanted behavior returning over and over, it's time to pay attention to it. Those things surface to teach us something about ourselves.

The key is to recognize that there is a pattern to them.

Thinking back on my recent experience, I thought I had put the issue to rest long ago. After all, I'm not one to walk away from introspection. Still, it became obvious, even to me, that I had not worked hard enough to resolve this issue. Now here it was, once again banging on my door. So this time I paid close attention and gave it a substantial amount of time and attention so I could finally resolve it and move on.

This wasn't easy. Resolving an issue never is. It requires us to take a hard look inside ourselves. It's much easier to look the other way and avoid hard-probing questions. Why do I do that? What can I do to stop? What am I supposed to learn from this? How can I be better? How is my pattern affecting others? What can I do to move on?

Ideally, we'll ask these questions of ourselves when we are younger. If we do, the issues won't exist when we're adults. But too often we don't do it because we don't know that we need to, and we don't know how.

Life is a journey, a continuous learning experience. It's not just about the world around us; it is about our inner world as well. How can we challenge ourselves to look inside when there are issues we need to deal with? I've learned that it's best to take that challenge, and when we do we are doing our greatest work. We gain a better sense of self. We build self-esteem and self-respect. We reinforce our personal truths.

We are not meant to glide along close mindedly in our thoughts and actions. We are meant to constantly learn about ourselves. Pretending that these patterns do not exist will not work. My little pattern was quiet for years. But it returned once again, asking me to resolve it. Finally, I was ready to do so, and I finished the lesson. It was difficult but worthwhile. In fact, it was essential.

If an issue surfaces, listen to it. It is our best teacher. It can surface at any age. If and when it does, have the courage to look deep within to resolve it.

Issues find ways to present themselves in our lives, and we are meant to learn from them. Let's embrace our issues — and discover how clear and light we will feel once we have done so.

Words of Wisdom

"Life is an ever-changing process, and nothing is final. Therefore, each moment and every new day is a chance to begin anew."

~Barbara Cage, greeting card author

First Impressions

We have only a few seconds to make a first impression.

As we approach someone new — immediately, instinctively — an opinion is formed, an assessment is made.

It is far easier to make a good first impression than to reverse a bad one.

The best way to make a good first impression is simply to smile. A sincere, genuine smile puts everyone at ease. A good, solid (but not bone-crushing) handshake and direct, deliberate eye contact are also important.

Before we can say a word, our appearance speaks volumes. Presenting ourselves appropriately begins with our dress. We must choose clothing that fits properly and is appropriate for the occasion. It's always a good idea to ask others what to wear when we will be in an unfamiliar situation.

Grooming is important, too. We want to show that we care about how we look — not as though we just jumped out of bed.

Timing matters, too, and that means being punctual. The first impression of a person dressed perfectly and acting properly will be ruined if he or she is late. No excuse matters. Tardiness equals disrespectfulness.

Pretending never works. We must just be ourselves. Take a deep breath before entering a room and just relax. Be comfortable with who we are, and don't try too hard. By being genuine, we are able to put people at ease.

We know who we are. We can share our knowledge when it's appropriate, but we don't need to overdo it. Just being open and confident is enough. The same is true for projecting a positive attitude. When we get nervous or face criticism, a positive outlook goes a long way.

Small talk matters — even if we don't like it. We should do some homework prior to meeting other people. Find out if we have common interests or hobbies. If we don't find any, just ask. People love people who ask questions!

Let others talk more. While in conversation be aware of how connected the others are to us. Have they tuned us out? We can tell by their body language. If they are distracted or fidgeting, it's time to move on.

We have only a few seconds to make a first impression, but it can last a lifetime. Let's make it a good one!

Notes to Notice

Be attentive, courteous, polite and engaged in conversation. Look at the eyes and mouth of the person who's talking to you. Don't look at other parts of the person's body or wardrobe unless you plan to quickly offer a compliment. Looking around the room as if bored is insulting, and texting or talking on a cell phone is worse. Being distracted doesn't make a good impression.

A Job Well Done

It is a tremendous gift to truly enjoy our profession every day. I am reminded of this by our firm's president, Ed Moore, who, as I write this, is celebrating his 20th anniversary with Edelman Financial Services.

Ric and I are so blessed to have crossed Ed's path 20 years ago, and our staff and clients are very lucky to have the talents and dedication of someone who truly loves what he does.

In 20 years with Edelman Financial Services, Ed has never taken a sick day. He comes to work with a smile on his face each day and gives each person and each task his full attention. Ed shows us that we honor ourselves when we do what we love.

Too often we come into contact with people who clearly are not happy with their jobs. They are easy to spot — there is no eye contact, listening skills are lacking and if a response is needed, it can be, well, snippy. It really shouldn't matter what we do for a living. We should have our minds and our hearts in our jobs.

When we do what we love, we easily and naturally give to those around us. When we do what we love, what we put into the job comes back to us tenfold. When we do what we love, we start each day with a smile and we treat everyone we encounter as we wish to be treated. It's easy when we do what we love.

It is not always easy to look at ourselves and ask hard questions.

"Am I doing the best I can do at this job?"
"Am I giving this job all that I have?"
"Have I learned all I can at this job?"
"Am I loving this job?"

These questions could cause us to conclude that it's time to rededicate ourselves to our job — or maybe that it's time to move on. If we decide it's time for a change, embrace that realization. Life is one long journey, and we are meant to try different things. We are meant to challenge ourselves and be open to changes. The goal is to "be" in our job with our hearts and our minds so we can honor ourselves and so we can honor those we work with and those we serve.

Life is a wonderful, rich journey if we will let it be. Don't close the floodgates — let the current take us where we need to go. Trust that the journey will give us the experiences we need so that at the next turn we are ready for what awaits us.

We are forever grateful that Ed's current led him to us. He is a wonderful example of someone who truly enjoys what he does. Our boat is a little bigger now, but we know the current will take us where we need to be, with him beside us at the helm.

Try It and See

List 3 things you love to do.

_____

_____

_____

Are you doing them?   Yes__   No__

What can you change to bring them back into your life?

Grab that calendar and find a small pocket of time to bring the activity back into your schedule.

Change Is Good

As I'm writing this, our neighborhood has just experienced an earthquake, a hurricane and floods. Wow, nothing like Mother Nature to help us realize that we don't control very much in our day! When Earth needs to change, it quakes. When Earth needs a good cleansing, it floods. Change happens all around us.

Why do we resist?

A small bit of change keeps the blood flowing. It creates a reason to get up in the morning. A little change makes today different from yesterday. Change challenges. Change keeps our minds open to possibilities.

Setting goals for change can happen when we need the change. The Earth changes every minute of every day. We can bring about change, too. Let's ponder some questions and invite change into our lives.

How would we like to change this year from last year? Were we kind to ourselves and others? Did we find enough free time? Did we find small ways to do something nice for someone whom we did not know? Did we communicate with loving words to those around us? Were we present and mindful in our day? Were we kind to ourselves with proper sleep, exercise and food? Did we find a way to enjoy and respect nature? Did we give back to people and animals not as fortunate? Did we begin each day with a clear intention of making it better? Did we save a bit more? Did we spend more time with those who are important to us? Did we get rid of the "busy" to free up time for more meaningful tasks? Did we step out of our comfort zone so we could get to know a bit more of what we are made of?

Answers to these questions will begin our path to change.

Sometimes, though, there are times when change is pushed upon us. These little roadblocks are opportunities to change — when we did not think we needed to do so. A roadblock is actually positive and a chance to reevaluate and move in a different direction.

For example, instead of driving to work, annoyed about traffic, we can be positive about the opportunity to change our normal commute. It might bring something wonderful into our day. We might hear our favorite song on the radio. We might be able to get in that extra call we needed to make (hands-free, of course). We might be able to spend a couple of more minutes in the car with the kids talking and learning about what is going on in their worlds. Just a small positive shift in our thinking — the willingness to be open to and positive about possibilities of change — can bring a whole new light to these daily roadblocks we see as inconveniences.

When we are stuck in a routine, inconveniences are a wake-up call. We would all be healthier if we could look at daily inconveniences as opportunities for change. We would be less stressed if we embraced these daily roadblocks as times to pause, think and move in other directions. We would have lower blood pressure if we took a positive view of the challenge and saw it as opportunity for change.

Let's make this our time to embrace change and see it in a more positive light. Try not to grumble or curse. Try a big belly laugh and a smile when roadblocks come our way.

Words of Wisdom

"The happiest people in the world are those who have a hard time recalling their worries…and an easy time remembering their blessings."

~Alin Austin, poet

Finding Joy

Do you find yourself anticipating the December holidays with excitement or dread? For many of us, the last month of the year finds us overextended, and the pressure of the season makes it worse. I can get tired just thinking about everything that needs to be accomplished.

We need to remember that the season is about the people, not the stuff. We also can help ourselves by planning, prioritizing and delegating.

Get a calendar and write down our commitments: what activities would we like to do vs. our commitments?

If we are hosting the family, when are they coming? When are they leaving? Plan activities in advance to keep them busy.

What decorating needs to be done? What meals need to be prepared? Can anything be cooked ahead of time and frozen? Restaurants and caterers can prepare and deliver meals.

If we are traveling, what will we need to take with us? What can we ship ahead of time?

Let's get realistic. Do we really need to knit a sweater for the cat?

Begin by admitting that we can't do everything for everyone. When we try to do too much, important activities get missed. Decide ahead of time the most important things that must be done. Give ourselves realistic time frames to finish them.

Let's remember that we don't necessarily have to be the ones to complete the task. Get the kids involved, and ask our spouse and relatives to help. It doesn't matter that they won't do it exactly the way we would. The point is that the task is getting completed, and we can check it off our list. We contribute to our stress when we act as though we are the only ones who can complete a project.

When family members do not perform as expected, keep your cool. Teach them how we do things so they can learn how to carry on family traditions. Ask them what they like best, and focus on those activities.

The joy we experience during the holiday season occurs because we are together with family and friends we love. The stuff is just fluff.

Don't let the year-end overwhelm us. Take control, have a plan and remember that it really is the season to be jolly.

Words of Wisdom

"Celebrate the happiness that friends are always giving, make every day a holiday and celebrate just living!"

~Amanda Bradley, greeting card author

Try It and See

Create a list of 3 items you would like to do differently this year-end. Who can help you complete the items?

_____

_____

_____

It's Not About the Stuff

Ever take the time to really look around?

Look, really look, around our home or office at all the items we have amassed. I often feel that all that stuff is nothing more than a burden requiring a lot of our time to care for — to clean, protect and insure.

When we are feeling overwhelmed by the stuff in our lives, it is often a little tap on the shoulder that it is time to merge or purge some items. Some items we hold onto so we can pass them to the next generation. Yet all we're really doing is passing along the burden of caring for, cleaning and protecting the items.

When we are young, we want everything. We think that "things" will bring us happiness and make us feel complete. As time goes on, we accumulate more and bigger items. But when we stop and look around, we still feel lost and incomplete. That's when we realize there has to be more to life than the "stuff" we've accumulated.

Ric and I were cured of materialism back in our mid-20s. We were weighed down with debt due to my medical bills. Determined to pay it off, we sold everything — even our television. After the yard sale, we packed the stuff that was left (what nobody wanted) into boxes and moved into a one-bedroom basement apartment. Because we had no furniture (having sold it all), we stacked our beloved boxes in the living room — we were too poor to afford a storage unit — and covered them with a sheet. And that's how we lived for five years, until we were debt-free and managed to build some savings. We were finally able to purchase our first home.

After we moved, the first thing we did was open all those boxes! We had nothing else to unpack. It had been five years since we'd packed away our precious stuff, and we were eager to return to it. What we found shocked us! We'd forgotten what the boxes contained and quickly realized that our lives had been fine without all of it, so we gave it all away. What a great lesson for us! We learned that it was nothing more than an illusion to think that the items stored in those boxes mattered.

Few would want to take the journey Ric and I traveled, but our path cured us of attaching importance to material things. We learned that what's important is each other and the people in our lives. Spending time with those who mean the most to us is the real treasure we should hold dear — not the stuff.

We now realize that stuff — our obsession to obtain stuff and then insuring and taking care of stuff — is, well, just stuff. And no matter how much we like our stuff, it doesn't like us back.

Owning stuff does not make us something we are not. Rather, who we are comes from within.

Let's spend less time with our stuff and more time with family and friends. Let's engage in activities that bring us together, make us laugh and appreciate one another. Examples might include game night, a picnic, or a walk with friends or family on a nice day.

After all, the greatest treasure is a life stuffed with memories that fill us with a smile, warmth and love.

Words of Wisdom

"Getting and spending, we lay waste our powers."

~Ralph Waldo Emerson (1803-1882), American essayist and poet

"Line your home with treasures and you won't be able to defend it."

~*The Tao Te Ching of Lao Tzu*, sage of the 6th century B.C.

The Secret to Mastering Your Calendar

The final months of the year are the most hectic. But if we are ready for them, we can flow through activities and upcoming events wearing smiles instead of gritting our teeth. The choice is ours: by being prepared, we can ride the wave, even though we'll get jostled a bit. Or we can be unprepared and find ourselves dashed upon the rocks as we futilely fight the waves.

So, let's prepare. Get a calendar and pull together all the sources that generate commitments for us: personal, work, relatives, friends, kids, spouse, school, holidays, charity, community and church. Create the entire list, get a big cup of tea and some colored pens — whatever we need to make the planning fun. List, by month, all the obligations and activities, and focus especially on the busiest months of the year.

As we quickly discover, we have far more requests and demands than we have time, money and ability to accommodate. That's where the secret to our calendar comes in: one simple, little word. Only two letters, spoken emphatically.

NO!

Too often we forget that we're allowed to decline invitations. When we learn to say no, we vastly improve our lives — and our family's lives — especially during busier times of year. Keep this in mind as you proceed.

Once we have laid out all the events, activities and duties being requested of us, we get a better idea of where the heavy blocks of time are. We can then begin to choose what we are going to do and where we need to commit ourselves. This will help us feel more in control.

1. **Start with our time** — Let's not forget that time for us is the most important commitment. Block out time in our morning, afternoon, late night — whatever is best. This is all ours!
2. **Then move to family time** — Set aside some evenings for dinner together and some for easy downtime.
3. **Work time** — Block out the business obligations that occur outside the normal workday.
4. **Children/school/sports** — Many children have heavier schedules than their parents do. Avoid overbooking activities for the kids — they need their downtime, too.
5. **Holidays** — They come every year, and we never seem to be ready. Allot time on our calendar now for shopping time, cooking time, wrapping time and travel time. This is a good opportunity to remember that we don't want to overspend, so adjust our calendar to avoid putting ourselves into situations that demand unnecessary spending.
6. **Friends/community/charity/church** — All need and deserve some time, and although our desires are infinite, the number of hours in a day is not. We must pick and choose and accept the fact that there are limitations. Decline, postpone or commingle — and say NO when you know you need (or want) to.

One important point to remember is that our calendar is never really complete. Obligations arise, schedules change, requests surface. Remain flexible but firm, and never agree to anything without first looking at our calendar to see if we can accommodate the new entry.

We always need to be flexible (but stay in control). Don't overdo it, learn to say NO — and enjoy!

Stress Reduction Strategies at Work

We all plan our calendar weeks or even months in advance. Trying to organize our future creates stress.

To reduce stress at work, we are not going to eliminate items from our calendar. Instead, we are going to *add* to it.

Add PRIVATE time — the same time each day.

This is a period each day when we simply will not answer the phone or see visitors. We need uninterrupted time to complete tasks — and to simply think and reflect. Look at your calendar right now and schedule an appointment with yourself. Start with a small amount of time — say, 15 minutes. As you grow accustomed to your private time you will want to increase it to 30 minutes or an hour. If someone tries to talk with you during this time, tell them you are unavailable.

Add PROBLEM RESOLUTION time.

Our days are packed, and everything is fine until something unexpected arises. Then we find ourselves double-booked, forced to be in two places at once or handling two issues simultaneously. This creates stress. The solution is simple: we need to leave time on our calendar for the unexpected. Then when problems erupt, we can respond without disrupting our entire day.

I learned how to handle such interruptions from my dentist. One day I had a bad toothache, so I called him. His assistant told me to come in at 11:30 that morning. When I got there, I thanked him for squeezing me into his calendar and apologized for interfering with his schedule, for I was certain that my emergency caused other patients to sit idly in his waiting room. "It's no problem at all," he said. "You're not causing any disruption to me or my other patients." Then he explained why: every day, someone calls needing to see him urgently. So, he explained, "I leave time on my daily schedule for emergencies, because I know that every day something will come up. I just don't know what it will be or when — all I know is that it will take 30-60 minutes to fix it." As a result, a patient's dental crisis doesn't become the dentist's scheduling crisis — and the patient's pain doesn't disrupt the schedule of the dentist or his other patients.

So now I do the same thing with my own calendar: I book time in my day to allow for unexpected problems that are certain to arise. I don't know what the problem will be or when it will hit — but I'm ready for it. This way, rather than having a problem interfere with my day, it simply becomes part of my day. As a result, problems are much less stressful, because I have given myself the time to resolve them without throwing the rest of the day into disarray.

Add PERSONAL time.

We have discovered that it takes 15 minutes to get a cup of coffee at work. We get up from our desk, go to the kitchen, clean our cup, fill it and return to our desk. Along the way, we encounter coworkers, resulting in impromptu hallway conversations. If we drink (or at least refill) four cups a day, we are spending one hour a day on coffee! We need to recognize this and schedule that time into our calendar.

Add time to ARRIVE EARLY.

I call this my get-stuck-in-traffic-without-exposing-myself-to-stress-over-being-late time. Plus, by getting there early, we might encounter a wonderful surprise awaiting us. We might get to meet someone who will make our day. If nothing else, arriving early gives us the chance to enjoy the private time we need.

Let's try scheduling time into our days for ourselves and the unexpected and see how much better we feel. We might see a great improvement in the quality of our lives.

Try It and See

Take one week in your calendar and add extra time for:

» Private time
» Problem resolution
» Personal time
» Time to arrive early

At the end of the week ask yourself if that extra time helped things feel less stressful. If so, add more of these to your calendar.

Words of Wisdom

"If you are distressed by anything external, the pain is not due to the thing itself but to your estimate of it; and this you have the power to revoke at any moment."

~Marcus Aurelius Antoninus (121-180 A.D.), Roman emperor and philosopher

Notes to Notice

Time Flies When We're Having Fun!

Where does the time go? What happened to all the time we had to finish all the projects? Why does the year seem to end so quickly?

Well, don't panic. Here are a few simple tips to help you feel better:

» Remember to take a moment and breathe.

» Keep some time for ourselves.

» Enjoy those around us. Stop thinking about the next task we need to complete.

» Let it go… If it is not perfect, we'll be the only one to notice.

» Don't feel we have to be the life of the party. Instead, sit back, observe, listen and watch — we will be very surprised.

» Less is better: overindulgence is never pretty. Savor, relish the moments and tastes.

» Great things come in small packages. Find meaningful gifts for the people on our list. And remember: meaningful does not have to mean expensive.

» Have patience. Especially at the busy times of year, when every thing takes longer. Plan extra time to get tasks done. The great thing is, what we did not get to finish this year we can look forward to finishing next year.

Giving Back

If we really think about it, all we are doing with our day is trading dollars. I pay you, and you turn around and pay someone else for their product or services. It is a cycle that has been in existence since the beginning of time.

In other words, what goes around comes around. What you sow, you reap. What you put into something is what you get out of it. The more you give, the more you receive. These truths need to be brought into our daily lives. Without them we lose the deeper meaning of life and the impact of our actions.

Ric and I find our biggest joy in our philanthropy. One-on-one time with the nurses we support. Visiting the planetarium when elementary schoolchildren are there and experiencing views of the solar system with kids seeing it for the first time. Visiting a shelter and helping deliver services for homeless children. Seeing first-hand the benefits of therapeutic horseback riding for wounded warriors and children with special needs. Moments like these, of hands-on giving back, are so enriching for the soul.

So the big question is: have we carved out any part of our day — and dollars — to give back to our community in some way? We can all do it.

Here are some ideas:

- Help out at a soup kitchen
- Mentor a young person
- Read to children at the library
- Support animals that are not so fortunate

- Support a national park
- Provide dinner for a sick friend
- Take an elderly neighbor grocery shopping
- Help a friend with a problem he or she is having
- Take a sick friend to his or her doctor appointments
- Volunteer at a school
- Help build a community garden
- Help a veteran or work with a wounded warrior

When our only goal is to obtain the most dollars for our time, we will never be fulfilled. We will always have a desire for something more. When there is empty desire with nothing to fulfill it, we make bad decisions and take the wrong path.

But when we give back, our life comes into better perspective.

What goes around comes around, and when we give to others we get far more than we give.

Words of Wisdom

"Spread love everywhere you go: first of all in your own house. Give love to your children, to your wife or husband, to a next-door neighbor… Let no one ever come to you without leaving better and happier. Be the living expression of God's kindness: kindness in your face, kindness in your eyes, kindness in your smile, kindness in your warm greeting."

~Mother Teresa (1910-1997), nun, Missionaries of Charity, Nobel Peace Prize winner

"What we do today, right now, will have an accumulated effect on all our tomorrows."

~Alexandra Stoddard, author and interior designer

How About You?

I hope you have enjoyed the journey of this book. I know some of it was not easy, but life is not always easy. We have the opportunity to change and learn every moment of every day. I hope you stay open for the changes that await you.

Through this book, I hope you found some little ways to reduce some of the stress in your life, feel more confident in nurturing meaningful relationships or just be able to find more laughter in your day. In all, I hope you've discovered more joy in your life and ways to share it with those around you.

So, the final challenge for this final week is to write down something that you've learned from reading over the past weeks. What was a special moment or experience you had? What is your *Other Side of Money*?

And if you're feeling especially outgoing...I invite you to share it with me. I'd love to hear *your* story.

You can e-mail me at stories@JeanEdelman.com.

Thoughts